# A One-Year Guide to the
*Catechism of the Catholic Church*

## GERRY RAUCH

CHARIS

SERVANT PUBLICATIONS
ANN ARBOR, MICHIGAN

Charis Books is an imprint of Servant Publications especially designed to serve
Roman Catholics.

Published by Servant Publications
P.O. Box 8617
Ann Arbor, Michigan 48107

99 00 01 02   10 9 8 7 6 5 4 3 2 1

Printed in the United States of America
ISBN 0-56955-026-3

LIBRARY OF CONGRESS CATALOGING-IN-PUBLICATION DATA

Rauch, Gerry.
    A one-year guide to the Catechism of the Catholic Church / Gerry Rauch.
        p.   cm.
    ISBN 1-56955-026-3 (alk. paper)
    1. Catholic Church.   Catechismus Ecclesiae Catholicae.   English.   2.
Catholic Church—Catechisms.   3. Devotional calendars.   I. Title.
BX1959.3.E5R38   1999
238'.2—dc21                                          98-48280
                                                     CIP

# INTRODUCTION
## How to Read the Catechism

Y ou are about to begin a project—reading the *Catechism of the Catholic Church* (the *Catechism*)—that will change your life. The ideas you will find in the *Catechism* are not ordinary ideas. They are the Church's explanation of what Christ revealed to us— thoughts that originate with God.

To put this another way, you interact with Christ when you read the *Catechism*. The thoughts the Church expresses here are his. Furthermore, the Church does not offer this book merely for academic interest, but to help you encounter Jesus Christ and become his disciple. You can meet him in the *Catechism* as you can meet him through the sacraments, through the Scriptures, through encounters with dedicated and holy Christians, and so on.

Therefore, it is helpful to ask how to best read the *Catechism*.

First of all, read it in a prayerful spirit. Since this is a book in which the Church explains what God has said to us, it is appropriate to approach it with your heart open to him in prayer. Even a brief prayer before you read will make your encounter with the *Catechism* much more meaningful.

Furthermore, since the *Catechism* is an expression of the mind of Christ, read it with expectation. Expect to hear him speaking about the meaning of your life, about his love for you, and about how he wants to save you. Expect him to tell you how he wants you to live.

As you read, expect to learn about Christ himself, about his Father, and about the gift of the Holy Spirit. Expect to learn about the Eucharist, and how to participate in it and the other sacraments. Expect to learn how to pray. If you are married, expect to learn how to build up love within your family. Expect to learn how to participate in society with a deeper understanding of the world events of the day.

Finally, read the *Catechism* with an intention to obey what you understand. Nothing else will make your reading as exciting as a determination to carry out what you learn. If you are reading the *Catechism* together with others in a discussion group, you will find it very helpful and encouraging to share with each other how you are applying what you learn.

To sum up: approach the *Catechism* in prayer, expecting that what the Church teaches about Christ in this book will open your mind in new ways—and then obey whatever you learn.

## Organization of *A One-Year Guide to the Catechism of the Catholic Church*

This *Guide* is organized to help you read through the entire *Catechism* in a year's time. About two pages of selections from the *Catechism* are presented for each day. There are seven days of readings for each of the fifty-two weeks of the year, covering the entire *Catechism*, with nothing repeated and nothing left out.

The selections for each Saturday—taken from the "In Brief" sections of the *Catechism*—are shorter, to give you a periodic break in your reading. These "In Brief" sections serve to review some of what you have read during the previous week.

For each day of the year, there are three elements to what the *Guide* presents. First are the numbers of the sections from the *Catechism* for the day's reading, combined with a brief list of some of the topics covered in those sections. Second, there is a short reflection that introduces the content of the readings. Finally, there is a short prayer for the day.

The list of topics for each day is not meant to present a complete picture of what is in the *Catechism* selections. Rather, combined with the reflection and the prayer, it is meant to give you a taste of what you will read in the *Catechism*. The three elements together should help you begin to focus on what is to follow. They are like an appetizer that sets the stage for the main course of the meal, which is the selection from the *Catechism.*

Thus, when you begin your reading each day, slowly and reflectively go through the list of topics in the book, then read the reflection and pray the prayer. This will help you slow down from the distractions of the day and enter into a prayerful attitude of reflection on the truths of the *Catechism* so that you will get the most out of what you read.

### Arrangement of the Readings From the *Catechism*

Sometimes the sections indicated for a day's readings are from one place in the *Catechism,* but more often they are from two, and sometimes three, different places.

Why should you read the *Catechism* in this kind of order instead of simply proceeding from front to back?

Obviously, reading from front to back is a fine pattern. But most readers will find their understanding and interest is enhanced by the liveliness that is created when the ideas from one part of the *Catechism* throw light on another part.

It's a little like reading the Bible. Most people find it difficult to read straight through from the Book of Genesis to the Book of Revelation. Similarly, the Church gives us selections from different parts of the Bible in each day's Scripture readings for the liturgy. It is usually easier, and more engaging, to read from different parts of the Bible as you proceed through it. As we consider the different selections together, they shed light on each other.

The groupings of readings from the *Catechism* in this *Guide* are meant to enrich your understanding by allowing you to see some of the many profound relationships between the different facets of the Church's teaching. Keep in mind that from day to day the selections fit together with different degrees of suitability. Sometimes they combine in ways that will give you remarkable insights. At other times, the result is less outstanding.

However, there will always be an abundance of material for reflection in each day's readings.

The sequence of the material from the *Catechism* in this *Guide* has a certain pattern to it. Each set of daily readings has a relationship to the material from the previous and following days. In general, you should find each day's readings naturally flowing from the ones before and naturally leading into the ones following. Topics will often recur in different places, but the overall pattern will be helpful for understanding. In fact, even if you were to read the *Catechism* from front to back, you would find topics recurring in various ways because of the interrelationship of all the truths God has revealed.

Finally, there are a few parts of the text in the *Catechism* that are not included under a section number. For instance, the scriptural text of each commandment is given before the first section number for that commandment. If you look at section 2084, for example, you will see that the text of the first of the Ten Commandments is given just before it. Whenever this kind of thing happens, read the text that is associated with a particular section even though it comes before the section number.

In summary, it is no exaggeration to say that through this incomparable document of the Church, the *Catechism*, you can grow in faith; you can find hope again; you can mature in love for God and neighbor. If you finish reading the entire *Catechism*, you will receive a solid and profound formation in the life of Christ that will continue to make a difference throughout your life.

April 9, 2000
Dec 2, 2001
Jan 2, 2005

27-30
We are created by God for God
Dignity of man: communion with God
God never ceases to call every person

2123-2126
Atheism: Restriction of one's vision to space and time
          Denial of dependence on God

Did we begin as a product of blind evolution? If so, the meaning of our lives is to contribute to moving the human race toward the next stage of evolution. Or did we fall from a former spiritual world into an evil material world? If so, the meaning of our lives is found when we are enlightened and thus freed from this evil material world. But if we came from the hand of God, then he is the meaning of our lives, and it is to him that we are called to return forever.

PRAYER: Father, help me take each step of life toward you, toward your truth and goodness.

## Monday Week 1

189-196
The baptismal creed
The truths of faith explained in reference to the Trinity
Different eras of history need different statements of the one
    creed

The Church summarizes what it believes through the creed. We even use the creed as a prayer, proclaiming the basic truths through which we have been saved, and through which we hope for eternal life.

PRAYER: Father, you sent your Son to reveal your truth to us. All you have taught us is holy and precious. Deepen our understanding that we might come closer to you.

---

## Tuesday Week 1

11-17

The *Catechism:* all the essentials of Catholic doctrine about faith and morals

Structure of the *Catechism:* profession of faith, sacraments, life in Christ, prayer

Today's *Catechism,* part of a heritage of truth, conversion, and holiness that goes all the way back to Christ

Throughout the centuries the Church has carefully guarded what God revealed. For our benefit, the Church in our day again gives us the full teaching of Christ in many ways. The *Catechism* is one of the most important of those ways.

PRAYER: Lord Jesus, I want to meet you in the teaching of your Church. I pray that you make yourself known to me as I read.

18-25
Explanation of cross-references, index, different sizes of print
*Catechism:* doctrine that changes lives
Adaptations of presentation: for different cultures, levels of
  maturity, and so on
All doctrine is directed toward a life of Christian love

Teaching about Christ is not meant to be an impersonal reflection on abstract truth, but a presentation of the Word of God, which always creates us anew. Through this process we become empowered to live lives that reflect his eternal love.

PRAYER: Father, I entrust my life to you. How can I grow in love unless you raise me up to be like yourself, you who are my true Father?

39-43
Man's ability to know God
Though unable to speak perfectly of God in human lan-
  guage, still we can say many things
214-217
God: He Who Is
God's love and faithfulness
God is Truth

The Fall began with the deception of Satan, the Father of Lies. Now it requires courage and love to find and hold on to the truth in the midst of a world with so much deception. In this battle Christ stays faithfully at our side.

PRAYER: Father, you are so great that we can only know you partially. But you have told us the truth by sending us Christ, who is the Truth. Help us to know you through him.

## Friday Week 1

2087-2094
Faith: source of moral life
Doubt, incredulity, heresy, apostasy, schism
Hope: confident expectation of divine blessing
Despair and presumption: sins against hope
God's divine charity and our response of love
Ingratitude, lukewarmness, hatred of God

1830-1832
Gifts and fruits of the Holy Spirit

Faith, hope, and charity allow us to relate directly to God—as true, as good, and as worthy of love. They are given to us at baptism as the heart of our new life in Christ.

PRAYER: O God, my hope, your Word is true. I know you love me with a love that will never fail. Fill my heart with love for you.

44-49

Man is a religious being, made to live in communion with
   God
Certainty about the existence of God
Spreading the knowledge of God to others

228-231

God is One
God is a mystery beyond words
God is Truth and Love

St. Augustine pursued the passing attractions of this world
but remained unsatisfied at heart. After God chose to reveal
himself to him, Augustine finally knew what he was made for:
"You have made us for yourself, and our hearts are restless
until they rest in you."

PRAYER: Father, we come from you and return to you.
Grant that we may return in forgiveness and love, to know
you and love you forever.

**105-114**

God is the author of Scripture; its human authors were
inspired by God

Christianity: religion of the living Word of God

The Holy Spirit opens our minds to understand Scripture

Key to interpreting Scripture: attention to what the human
authors intended and what God wanted to reveal

God's Word far surpasses our powers to fully comprehend
it. The goal of the Christian is not to master it but to be mastered by it. For God's Word, which created the world, now
makes us a new creation in Christ.

PRAYER: Lord Jesus Christ, speak your Father's Word to me
that I might become his child in you. You came to restore all
creation to God's intention; restore me in your love.

**101-104**

Sacred Scripture: the Word of God

God speaks to us in human words

God's one unique Word: Christ

**131-133**

Theology and preaching: based on Sacred Scripture

Read Scripture frequently

**2762-2764**

The Lord's Prayer at the center of the gospel

The Word of God in Scripture has the power to change human life. It is a book of life, the new life in Christ that is fully human and befitting creatures of God.

PRAYER: Lord, change our hearts and our minds as we hear your Word of Life.

## Tuesday Week 2

115-119
Literal and spiritual senses of Scripture
Allegorical sense: the events of Scripture as signs or types of Christ and Christianity
Moral sense: the events of Scripture lead us to act justly
Anagogical sense: the realities and events of Scripture point toward eternity

128-130
Unity of the Old and New Testaments
The two Testaments: each valuable on its own, each illuminated by the other

Too often have people reduced the Scriptures to the level of other literature. This closes the door to what God wants to give us through his living Word. A renewal of the Church's approach to Scripture returns us to the wellspring of our life in God.

PRAYER: Lord, I love your Word. Through it you show me the depths of my own soul and your great love that saves me from all that is wrong.

120-127
Canon: which books are part of Scripture
The Old Testament prepares for the New Testament
New Testament: centrality of Jesus Christ
The unique place of the Gospels in the Church

Out of all the Scriptures, the New Testament is most important. Among the books of the New Testament the four Gospels occupy first place. It is here that we meet Christ in the most profound way, so that we may believe in him and have life in his name.

PRAYER: Father, with St. Paul, give me the grace to be able to say, "I am not ashamed of the gospel: It is the power of God for salvation to every one who has faith" (Rom 1:16).

577-582
Jesus came not to abolish the Law but to fulfill it
Many in Israel were zealous for the Law
The Law written on the heart
Jesus was seen as a rabbi, and he taught with authority

God never wanted us to act against our fellow human beings, and so Jesus repeated the commandment against killing. But he also pointed out that God intends that we not commit even lesser offenses like anger or disdain. Thus Jesus' interpretation of the Law disclosed God's full intention in giving the Law.

PRAYER: Father, your righteousness stands firm forever. We love your commandments, which set us free from error.

---

## Friday Week 2

---

**583-586**

Jesus respected the temple in Jerusalem as his Father's house

Jesus announced the coming destruction of the temple as part of the coming of a new age in salvation history

**797-798**

The Holy Spirit joins all parts of the Church into one with Christ the head

The Holy Spirit is the principle of every saving action in each part of the Body of Christ

God revealed himself to Israel as one who dwelt in their midst in the temple. His presence with them signaled that they were the Chosen People. Now in Christ, God dwells not just in a physical tabernacle but in each follower of Christ by the presence of the Holy Spirit.

PRAYER: Jesus Christ, you promised that you would send your Holy Spirit to be with us until you return in glory. Give us the Spirit's presence all the days of our lives.

134-141
Scripture is the inspired Word of God
Interpretation of Scripture must be attentive to God's intent
Centrality of the four Gospels
Unity of Old and New Testaments

592-594
Jesus fulfilled the Old Law and revealed its meaning
The temple's relationship to Jesus

We would go out of our way to hear a word that God addressed to us personally. Yet he has done just that in the Scriptures. The Scriptures are his Word to us today just as much as they were his Word during the times of the Old and New Testaments.

PRAYER: Lord, you said your Word would not return to you empty but that it would accomplish what you sent it to do. May it accomplish the new life in me that you intend.

**1213-1216**

Through baptism we are freed from sin; reborn as sons of God and members of Christ

Baptism is called: washing of regeneration, renewal by the Holy Spirit, enlightenment

**1328-1332**

The sacrament of the Body and Blood of Christ is called: Eucharist, Lord's Supper, Breaking of Bread, Eucharistic assembly, memorial, Holy Sacrifice, Holy and Divine Liturgy, Holy Communion, Holy Mass

Baptism is the sacrament that opens the door to all the other sacraments, and the Eucharist is the high point of the sacraments. Both are so rich and so profound that they can be considered from many different perspectives, and thus they have many different names. Their depth is so great that it is beyond our full grasp.

PRAYER: Lord, you have come into our midst to remain with us until we arrive with you in heaven. We exalt in your glory.

**1217-1222**

Old Testament prefigurations of baptism: Noah's Ark, Crossing the Red Sea, Crossing the Jordan River

Water, source of life and fruitfulness

Waters of death

1333-1336

The Eucharist foreshadowed in the Old Testament

In Jesus' life: multiplication of loaves; water changed into wine at Cana

The realities of the life of Jesus in the New Testament were prefigured in the Old Testament. It is like the casting of a shadow—the outlines of the life and sacrifice of Christ were already visible in some ways in the time of preparation—but the full reality is only visible when it is revealed in Jesus Christ.

PRAYER: Lord, you promised your first coming as you now promise your second coming. Let your light shine on us until the day when we see you face to face.

---

## Tuesday Week 3

---

1229-1233

Various approaches to Christian initiation throughout the centuries

Infant baptism requires a postbaptismal catechumenate

RCIA: Rite of Christian Initiation of Adults

1655-1658

Believing families: centers of radiant faith

Parents: first to announce the faith to their children

The Christian home is the environment where those baptized as infants usually first hear about the Christian life and receive a formation in it. Thus there is an essential link between Christian life in the home and the sacraments of the

Church. Therefore the pastors of the Church are especially interested in the way of life lived in each Christian home.

PRAYER: Lord, be gracious to our families. Come and live with us as we seek to honor you in our lives.

---

## Wednesday Week 3

1246-1252
Anyone not yet baptized can be baptized
Catechumenate: formation in the whole Christian life
Infant baptism was practiced from the earliest days of the Church

1306-1311
Every baptized person should receive confirmation
Preparation for confirmation
Confirmation sponsor

Baptism and confirmation are like two parts of the same reality. When we share the life of Christ by baptism we also share the life of his Holy Spirit. Thus in adult baptism the person also receives confirmation at the same time.

PRAYER: Lord Jesus Christ, give us your Spirit always. May your life increase in us and may everything else decrease.

---

## Thursday Week 3

1253-1256
Baptism: threshold of a new life that must grow
Godfathers and godmothers

Ordinary ministers of baptism: bishops, priests, deacons
In case of necessity, anyone may baptize

1262-1264
Immersion in water: sign of purification and new birth
Original sin and all personal sins forgiven in baptism

The word *baptism* comes from a Greek word meaning immersion—for example, a complete immersion into water. Thus, for us baptism is a complete immersion into Christ—into his death on the cross, into his risen life, into his Holy Spirit.

PRAYER: Lord Jesus, you took away our shame through the cross, by including us in your death and resurrection. We praise you for your abundant mercy.

---

## Friday Week 3

---

456-460
God so loved the world that he gave his only Son
The Word became flesh to be our model of holiness and to make us partakers of the divine nature

1265-1266
Baptism makes us new creatures, partakers of divine nature
Baptism gives us sanctifying grace, enabling us to believe in God, hope in him, and love him

Our destiny in Christ is hard to fully comprehend. God wants us to share his own life by being incorporated into his Son through faith and baptism. We have become children of God already, and all that means will be fully visible when we rise from the dead in Christ.

PRAYER: Father, we offer ourselves to you freely to become your children in Christ. We praise you for sending him to us.

## Saturday Week 3

1275-1284
Christian initiation: baptism, confirmation, Eucharist
Baptism: forgiveness of sins and new life in Christ
Baptism is necessary for salvation
Indelible sign of baptism
Baptism of desire

As the waters of the Red Sea swallowed up Pharaoh, so the waters of baptism engulf the evil of our state of sin. And as the Israelites were delivered through the Red Sea, so we are ushered into new life through baptism. Thus, in baptism, water is a sign both of the death of what is evil in us and of the new life we enter with Christ.

PRAYER: Father, maker of heaven and earth, you remake us in your Son. You give us new hearts to praise you; your great mercy endures forever.

**1127-1130**

The sacraments confer the grace they signify

Christ is at work in the sacraments

*Ex opere operato*

**1581-1584**

The sacrament of Holy Orders makes the priest able to act
as a representative of Christ

Unworthiness of the minister does not prevent Christ from
acting

Christ, who ascended to God's right hand, is now
present everywhere in his Church and personally acts on
our behalf. He does this in a real though mysterious way
through his Word and in the sacraments. Though we do
not see him directly, it is really he who meets us in the
ministry of his Church.

PRAYER: Jesus Christ, I welcome and receive you. I open
my heart to be obedient to your Word. Fill my life with
your presence.

**1210-1212**

Christ instituted the seven sacraments

Resemblance between the stages of natural life and the stages
of spiritual life

The sacraments form an organic whole, with the Eucharist at
the center

1113-1116

Jesus' words and actions had saving power, which is now
  present in the sacraments
The sacraments come forth from the Church, the body of
  Christ

The sacraments contain and unfold the same grace and power that was present when people encountered Christ in person. When we come to the sacraments we come to him, we encounter his saving words and deeds. By faith we receive what Christians have always received through this encounter: life in Christ.

PRAYER: Come, Holy Spirit, open the eyes of our hearts to meet Christ in the Eucharist, in penance, and in all the sacraments.

## Tuesday Week 4

355-361

God created man in his own image
Called to share by knowledge and love in God's own life
The dignity of the person and communion of persons
The mystery of man becomes clear only in the light of the
  mystery of the Word made flesh

In a way that reflects the communion of three persons in one God, humanity, though made up of so many individuals, has a unity as one race. But ultimately mankind's unity can be achieved only as we enter into and share the one life of love within the Trinity.

PRAYER: Lord God, you bring all mankind back into one through your Church. Give us the love for our neighbor that will enable us to be instruments of your work in this world.

---

## Wednesday Week 4

362-368

The human person willed by God is at once corporeal and
  spiritual
Soul: the spiritual principle in man
The body shares in the dignity of the image of God
Every soul is created immediately by God and is immortal

The unity of the soul and the body makes the person human. Our life now is spiritual and material, and our life in heaven will also be spiritual and material. Our bodies will rise again, and even though we don't know what they will be like, we do know that we will be like Christ because we will be members of his body.

PRAYER: Lord, care for us on this earth, and raise us up after death to fully share your life.

---

## Thursday Week 4

374-379

Paradise before the Fall: friendship with God and harmony
  with each other and with creation
The new creation in Christ surpasses Paradise

1718-1719
The Beatitudes reveal the goal of human existence
The Beatitudes respond to the natural desire for happiness

It is hard to imagine the wonders of Paradise where Adam
and Eve dwelt in harmony within themselves, with each
other, and with all creation. They also shared a close relationship with God. Yet we believe that the new creation in Christ
will lift us to a higher state than they enjoyed before the Fall.

PRAYER: How glorious is your dwelling place, Lord God of
all creation. Hold us fast that we may return to you as you
always intended.

---

## Friday Week 4

---

1-3
Life of man: to know and love God, to share God's life
God calls to man, drawing all into the unity of his Church

1699-1700
Life in the Holy Spirit fulfills the vocation of man
The dignity of the human person is rooted in his creation in
    the image and likeness of God
Freedom of the human person

The life of Christ in us is the central mystery of Christianity. Thus St. Paul can say, "It is no longer I who live, but
Christ who lives in me" (Gal 2:10). Encountering Christ,
and through him the Father and the Holy Spirit, gives us the
key to human life and restores us to what God intended for
mankind.

PRAYER: Lord Jesus Christ, you are the Good Shepherd who leads us to springs of living water. You are the pearl of great price, for which we sell everything else.

## Saturday Week 4

380-384
Mankind is made in the image and likeness of God
Each soul is created directly by God
Partnership of man and woman: first form of communion
  between persons

1710-1715
The human person is made for happiness with God
Freedom: manifestation of the divine image

The dignity of every human being consists in the fact that he or she is created by God, for God. Since the sin of Adam and Eve, we are all wayward sons and daughters of a great Father. But we can be restored to God's friendship by the Holy Spirit and regain our great dignity before God.

PRAYER: Lord God, what is man that you are mindful of him? You created us in order to share your own life with us. Your plan of love is greater than we ever could have imagined.

**484-486**
Jesus, conceived by the power of the Holy Spirit
The Annunciation inaugurated the fullness of time

**689-690**
Joint mission of the Son and of the Spirit
The Spirit is truly God
Mission of the Spirit: to unite God's children to Christ

The Holy Spirit does not draw attention to himself but shows us the Father in the glory of Christ. The indwelling of the Holy Spirit in our hearts unites us to Christ so that we are truly his body on this earth. The one Spirit in every Christian throughout the earth unites the Church so that it is one.

PRAYER: Come, Holy Spirit, and live in our hearts that we might be fully united to Christ and fully immersed in his mission for the salvation of the earth.

**721-726**
Mary conceived without sin
Communion with Christ through Mary
Mary, the New Eve

**2673-2675**
Mary's consent in faith at the Annunciation and at the foot
of the Cross

Mary's motherhood extended to the brothers and sisters of her Son

Mary's role in salvation and in the Church is unique. She is the Mother of all who are members of her Son. All generations have called her blessed.

PRAYER: Remember, O most gracious virgin Mary, that never was it known that anyone who fled to your protection, implored your help, or sought your intercession was left unaided. Inspired by this confidence, we fly to you, O virgin of virgins our Mother; to you we come, before you we stand, sinful and sorrowful. O Mother of the Word incarnate, despise not our petitions, but in your mercy hear and answer us.

---

## Tuesday Week 5

---

2676-2679
The Hail Mary
Mary, God's humble servant, full of grace
With Elizabeth all generations call Mary blessed
We trust all our cares to Mary, our mother

Catholics are led by the Holy Spirit to turn to Mary in prayer. Though some Christians question this practice, those who turn to Mary testify to the great blessings they receive. Honoring Mary with our prayers honors Christ, whom she always presents to the world.

PRAYER: Hail, Mary, full of grace. The Lord is with you. Blessed are you among women, and blessed is the fruit of your womb, Jesus.

966-971

The Assumption: Mary taken body and soul into heaven
Mary our mother in the order of grace
Mary's intercession for us in heaven
Devotion to the Blessed Virgin Mary

As he was dying on the cross, the Gospel of John tells us, Jesus pronounced Mary's motherhood of his disciples. We are all included in that relationship to her; her care for men and women extends as far as does the work of her Son.

PRAYER: Holy Mary, Mother of God, pray for us sinners now and at the hour of our death.

669-670

Christ dwells on earth as the head of the Church, and he exercises authority over it
The final age of the world is with us

787-791

The Church is communion with Jesus; we are associated with his own life, mission, joy, and sufferings
Diversity of members in the one body, which triumphs over all human divisions

The Lord not only unites different individuals in himself, he also unites different societies and cultures. Now that he is risen he accompanies us throughout history till the end of the world. His great love now endures with us and makes us one with him.

PRAYER: Lord Jesus, we believe that we share your life. How great is our joy! And how great it will be when we see you face to face!

---

## Friday Week 5

---

675-679

Before Christ's second coming the Church will pass through a final great trial

The Antichrist, by which man will glorify himself in place of God and God's Messiah

The Last Judgment: the conduct of each person and the secrets of hearts revealed

2855-2856

Christ will restore all to the Father

Amen

The Lord's warnings about the trials before the end of the world are so severe that we must be entirely sober about our lives and the life of the Church. Pursuit of holiness and imitation of Christ are the only adequate responses.

PRAYER: Lord, come quickly. Our world longs for you, and for the glory of the Father that you bring. All honor and glory belong to you.

680-682
Christ's reign is real now but a last assault of evil will come
before it is complete
Second Coming of Christ; Judgment

1795-1802
Right conscience and erroneous conscience
Guidance of the Word of God

God will lay bare the heart of every person when Jesus comes again. Then we will be glad for every moment of our lives when we followed the guidance of our consciences, and ashamed of every moment when we did not.

PRAYER: Lord Jesus, since the world will come to an end, we want to live for the things of heaven, which will last forever. When you come again, have mercy on all who have served you faithfully.

391-395
Satan, Father of Lies, murderer from the beginning
Satan led our first parents into sin
The Son of God appeared to destroy the works of the devil
Satan's power is not infinite; he is only a creature

2850-2854
Evil is not an abstraction; Satan is a person, the Evil One
Satan: deceiver of the whole world

Men and women in a state of harmony with God in Paradise did not sin on their own. God's enemy, out of envy, seduced mankind to follow his ways. But God's love overcame Satan's evil and we can now return to harmony with God.

PRAYER: Deliver us, Lord, we beseech you, from every evil, so that by your mercy we might be ever free from sin.

1852-1860
The different kinds of sin
The works of the flesh
Sin is rooted in the human heart
Mortal sin: grave violation of God's law, destroying charity in the heart
Venial sin wounds and offends charity in the heart

Human beings are able to deliberately offend God their Creator and Lord to such an extent that they lose the life of grace. Sin that is this serious is called mortal, or deadly. But we can return from the death of sin by God's grace.

PRAYER: Lord God, in your mercy blot out my sins. Cleanse me so that I may again be pleasing to you.

## Tuesday Week 6

### 1861-1864

In our freedom we are capable of mortal sin, which excludes us from Christ's kingdom

Grave offense is outwardly recognizable, but judgment of the person is left to God

Venial sin: less serious matter or lack of full knowledge or consent

### 1455-1458

All mortal sins must be confessed

One aware of unconfessed mortal sin must not receive Communion until absolution is received

Sacramental confession of our sins to a priest restores us to the life of grace if our sins are mortal. It strengthens the life of grace in us if the sins are venial. In the person of Christ, the priest absolves our sins and we are made new.

PRAYER: Deliver me from my guilt, O God, in your mercy. Restore me to the fullness of life with you.

1033-1037
Hell: State of definitive self-exclusion from communion with
  God
The wide way leads to destruction
God predestines no one to hell
Mortal sins lead to hell
The Church implores the mercy of God

We are created to live forever and will do so either in
God's presence in joy, or away from his presence in suffering.
Living wisely means shaping our daily thoughts and actions
in light of this truth about our destiny.

PRAYER: Lord, deliver me from the fires of hell. Lead all souls
to heaven, especially those in greatest need of your mercy.

## Thursday Week 6

1023-1029
Heaven, our greatest happiness and our true identity
Beatific vision: to see God as he is, face to face
To be with Christ, Mary, the saints, and the angels

2794-2796
Heaven: God's majesty, God's dwelling place
Christ descended from heaven and causes us to ascend there
  with him

We look forward to an eternal life in heaven that is more

than we could ever ask for. There we will be like Christ, for we shall see him face to face, as he is.

PRAYER: O God, grant that we may praise you forever with all your saints and angels.

---

## Friday Week 6

279-281
God: Creator of heaven and earth
Creation: foundation of all God's saving plans
Christ illuminates God's intention for creation

1042-1045
The hope of the new heaven and the new earth
God will dwell among men; unity of the human race

The Father created the world with his Son in mind. Even from the beginning, God's intention was that creation would find its meaning and fulfillment in Christ. Then when sin intervened through the fall of our first parents, Christ was sent to save us. Now we await the fulfillment of God's plan, when every tear will be wiped away. Then, in a new earth and a new heaven, God's original intention for creation will be fulfilled.

PRAYER: Father, how you love us that you did not leave us in our sins, but sent your Son for our redemption. May you be eternally blessed and praised!

1051-1060
Resurrection from the dead
Judgment
Heaven, purgatory, hell
Prayer for the dead

After death all men and women face God's judgment, which leads ultimately to eternity in either heaven or hell. The Church also teaches us that those who are saved but not yet perfected pass through purgatory in preparation for heaven. It is an act of love to remember souls who may be in purgatory by offering prayers and sacrifices on their behalf.

PRAYER: God, what our eyes have never seen, what our ears have never heard, you have prepared for us—more than we could ask or imagine.

**1010-1014**

The positive meaning of Christian death

"For to me to live is Christ, to die is gain"

In baptism we have died with Christ

Physical death completes the Christian's incorporation into Christ

We die once; there is no reincarnation after death

Preparing for death

Death is an awesome reality in each person's life. We know what lies beyond death only by faith; yet there lies our destiny for all eternity. In the face of such a daunting truth it is trust in our loving Father that sustains us. His desire for our good surpasses even our own.

PRAYER: St. Joseph, as Jesus and Mary attended you at the time of your death, I turn to you to pray for me at the hour of my own death.

**954-956**

Three states of the Church: on earth, in purgatory, in heaven

The intercession of the saints

**1030-1032**

Purgatory: purification after death, achieving the holiness necessary for heaven

Prayers and offerings on behalf of the dead

How different must be the perspective of those who belong to Christ who are already in heaven! Surely they would encourage us to recall what Christ said: "In the world you will have trouble. But be not afraid for I have overcome the world." And just as we would want to be remembered if we were in purgatory, so out of love should we remember to pray for those who have died.

PRAYER: Pray for your loved ones who have died, that God may bring them quickly to be with him in heaven.

---

## Tuesday Week 7

---

388-390

The Fall: a deed that took place at the beginning of the history of man

The Holy Spirit convicts us of sin by revealing Christ the Redeemer

1849-1851

Sin: offense against reason and truth, offense against God

In Christ's Passion, sin most manifests its violence and evil, and is then defeated

As salvation history progressed to the point of Jesus' Passion and death, the contrast between the light of God and the darkness of sin increased. Who would think that we men and women would judge our Creator worthy of punishment and death? How great is God's mercy to overcome our "culture of death" with his new life!

PRAYER: Father, evil for all its darkness flees before your light. Shine in my heart and create me anew.

397-401
Man's first sin consisted of disobedience and lack of trust
Man preferred himself to God
The entrance of death into human history

1865-1867
Sin creates an increased tendency to sin
Vices and capital sins

The sin of our first parents opened the door to an entire history of evil. By God's grace, however, evil in our world is restrained because he intends to offer us his mercy. Immediately after the Fall, in addition to telling Adam and Eve the consequences, he promised to send a Redeemer.

PRAYER: Have mercy on me, O God, forgive my sins and give me the grace to be faithful to you.

## Thursday Week 7

976-983
"I believe in the forgiveness of sins"
Faith and baptism for the forgiveness of sins
The weakness of nature remains after complete forgiveness of
    sins at baptism
Sins after baptism and the sacrament of Penance

The glory of God is revealed in a unique way in the forgiveness of sins. Even our rejection of him and the evil that follows are not too great an obstacle for him to overcome. He brings good out of our evil. If, by his grace, we turn to him in repentance, then he is glorified as a uniquely loving Father.

PRAYER: Father, you rescued me when I did not deserve it. What great love you show me through Christ your Son.

---

## Friday Week 7

---

1005-1009

At death the soul is separated from the body, to be reunited at the resurrection
Death: wages of sin; shadow of doubt over mankind
Christian death: participation in the death of Christ
God destined man to live forever

1021-1022

Different final destinies: each person receives the eternal consequences of his life at the moment of death

The Scripture tells us that even though we die in Adam, we will be brought to life in Christ. And even though we will eventually return to life in the resurrection, now there is no way to avoid the pain of death. Yet Christians face death with hope. For we know that death is not the end.

PRAYER: Lord, grant me the grace at the moment of my death to have the joy of confidence in your forgiveness, and confidence that I will rise in Christ and be with you forever.

984-987
The power to forgive sins given to the apostles and their successors
Sins are forgiven in baptism

1870-1876
All have sinned; sin is rooted in the heart
Mortal sin and venial sin

Sin is a grave reality in everyone's life. Some are hardened in their wrongdoing and do not care. Others know they have sinned and are unhappy until their sins can be removed by the Lord through the words of the priest: "I absolve you from your sins."

PRAYER: Father, I have sinned against you through my own fault. Hear my prayer of repentance and receive me in your mercy.

1391-1395

Holy Communion augments our union with Christ

The Eucharist strengthens our charity, which tends to weaken in daily life

The Eucharist preserves us from future mortal sins

1524-1525

The Eucharist as viaticum at the time of our death

At the time of death we also receive Penance and the sacrament of anointing of the sick

The Eucharist restores and builds up our entire life in Christ. The presence of Christ and his work of salvation in this sacrament are the reasons we make a special effort to approach the sacrament in a holy manner.

PRAYER: Lord, you have given us a remarkable gift, in that we can turn to you daily in the Eucharist. You are always present to satisfy our spiritual hunger for eternal food.

547-550

Miracles, healing, casting out evil spirits: all invite faith in Christ

Some are offended by Jesus' power

Jesus did not come to abolish all evils here below, but to free us from sin

1506-1508
Christ's followers, associated with his poverty and service
Signs worked by the Church
Spiritual charism of healing

Miracles and healings have been present in the Church
since the times of Scripture. Our rational and scientific age
has lost its expectation of God's intervention, but Christ still
reaches out by the power of the Holy Spirit in response to
the faith of his little ones.

PRAYER: Lord, multiply your wonders in our time as by a
new Pentecost, that more and more souls may turn to you.

---

## Tuesday Week 8

---

1420-1424
We are subject to suffering, illness, death, and sin
The Church continues Christ's healing and salvation in the
    sacraments of Penance and Anointing of the Sick

1499
Anointing of the sick: the Church commends the ill to the
    suffering and glorified Christ

1511-1513
The sacrament of the sick: to strengthen those tried by ill-
    ness; Extreme Unction

As we continue to follow the Lord through this world of
trials, we encounter times when we need physical or spiritual
healing. Through Christ's mercy, the Church reaches out to

us in those times—rescuing us from spiritual death through the sacrament of Penance and comforting us in illness and death through the sacrament of the sick.

PRAYER: Deliver us, O Lord, from suffering; preserve us from evil. May your mercy come quickly.

---

## Wednesday Week 8

**1500-1505**
Illness: one of the gravest problems of life; glimpse of death
Illness leads us to turn toward God or away
Redemptive meaning of suffering
The most radical healing: victory over sin and death

**1509-1510**
The Church is charged to heal the sick by care and intercession

The mystery of evil touches us and our loved ones in this life. Seldom are we told why we suffer, but God does not want the evil to lead us away from him. He calls us to keep our eyes on him as our Savior.

PRAYER: O God, deal bountifully with me as your servant so that I may live a life of obedience and faith in you.

---

## Thursday Week 8

**1514-1519**
The sacrament of the sick is not a sacrament only for those at the point of death

2288-2291
Life and health are gifts of God
The neo-pagan cult of the body
Avoid excesses of food, alcohol, tobacco, medicine
On the use of drugs

Bodily health is one of our earthly concerns. When it is seriously endangered, the Church cares for us through the sacrament of anointing. Just as Christ did in the New Testament, his Church reaches out to meet our needs when we experience physical suffering.

PRAYER: Father, I trust you for my earthly journey. Give me the health I need to serve you.

---

## Friday Week 8

---

624-627
Christ tastes death: "I died, and behold I am alive evermore"
Christ's body preserved from corruption

1680-1683
The Christian meaning of death revealed in Christ's death and resurrection
The Church commits the Christian to the earth as a seed that will rise in glory

Christ's death and ours are mysteries that we understand only by faith. What appears as a defeat is really a transition to a new state of life. When we rise from the dead at the end of time it will be with a completely new body, new in the way Christ's was when he rose.

PRAYER: Deliver me, O Lord. Preserve me from death and all evil.

---

## Saturday Week 8

629-630
Christ tasted death
Christ's body did not experience corruption

1526-1532
Sacrament of anointing of the sick, given when a person is in
    danger of death
The rite and graces of this sacrament

There is an incomparable consolation for the dying person, and for his or her family, when the sacrament of anointing of the sick is received at the time of death. For this is the time when we set off on a journey shrouded in mystery. The sacrament assures us that it is a journey that Christ pioneered for us, leading to a new life.

PRAYER: Lord Jesus, you have shown us the way through death to new life. We keep our eyes fixed on you as a light in the midst of darkness.

**595-596**
The Jewish authorities were divided concerning Jesus
The Sanhedrin declared Jesus deserving of death

**599-600**
Jesus was handed over to die according to God's plan
God's eternal plan foresaw and permitted the acts against Jesus

Jesus could have avoided death by use of his divine power against his enemies. The fact that he did not indicates that his death was God's will. And so now we believe that his death destroyed death, a far greater victory than any temporary earthly triumph.

PRAYER: Lord Jesus, we always recall your words and deeds. They shed light on our lives and give us hope. Your way alone is holy.

**410-412**
God did not abandon mankind after the Fall
Christ, the New Adam; Mary, the New Eve
Why did God not prevent the Fall?

**606-607**
Christ's whole life is an offering to the Father
Christ's redemptive passion was the reason for his Incarnation

From beginning to end, Christ has dominated history.

God's intent to make all mankind one in him leads us to call him the New Adam. We are destined to share in his life and in his eternal glory.

PRAYER: Father, you gave us Jesus Christ as our Lord and Savior. In spite of our sins, have mercy on us for the sake of your Son's honor and glory.

---

## Tuesday Week 9

---

604-605
God's initiative to redeem us out of love; we did not merit salvation
God's love excludes no one

1076-1078
Outpouring of the Holy Spirit at Pentecost: beginning of a new era, the age of the Church
Christ now lives and acts in and with his Church
The sacraments: communication of the fruits of Christ's Paschal mystery

Just as God created us without previous merit on our part, so he makes us new in Christ not on the basis of our merit but as a free gift of grace. As much as we would like to find some reason on our part for God's choice, there is none. We can only contemplate his free choice in awe, and worship him in thanksgiving for his great love.

PRAYER: Father, the wonders of your love are too much for me. I will be eternally grateful to you.

608-609
The Lamb of God who takes away the sin of the world
Christ's mission: to give his life as a ransom for many
Jesus Christ freely accepted his Passion and death

2838-2841
Forgive us our trespasses as we forgive those who trespass
  against us.

Jesus tells the parable of the servant who was forgiven a great sum that he could not repay. The servant, in turn, would not forgive his neighbor a small sum. We are all great debtors to God. And even if our fellow human beings are in debt to us, still they owe us so much less than we owe to God.

PRAYER: God of mercy and kindness, I am not worthy of your forgiveness. I forgive others the wrongs they have done to me. Please forgive my great offenses against you.

610-612
Last Supper: Jesus' anticipation of the offering of his life
"This is my body.... This is my blood"

1337-1340
Institution of the Eucharist at the Last Supper
Jesus, the Bread of Life

Israel celebrated the Passover after God set them free from Egypt. Jesus took that same celebration and transformed it into his own Passover meal, which sets us free from our sinful world to enter the Promised Land of heaven.

PRAYER: Lord, as the psalm says, you have indeed prepared a table for me. Surely goodness and kindness will follow me, and I shall dwell in your house forever.

## Friday Week 9

### 618

The cross is Christ's unique sacrifice, but he unites himself with us in it

Christ's mother: most intimate participant in his redemptive suffering

### 628

Baptism: to die with Christ in order to live with him

### 1226-1228

Since its beginning the Church has celebrated baptism

Baptism: putting on Christ

Just as all mankind was joined to Adam, so all mankind can be joined to Christ. Baptism is the sacrament that signifies and accomplishes this participation in Christ. But it calls for us to be conformed to Christ's death as well as to his new life.

PRAYER: Lord Jesus, you are my portion in life. Hold me fast, by your grace, to live as you lived.

619-623
Christ died for our sins
Salvation is an initiative of God's love

1015-1019
Resurrection of the body
Death is a consequence of sin
Christ's death conquered death

Mankind judged Jesus worthy of death. Yet he prayed, "Father, forgive them; for they know not what they do" (Lk 23:34). How true it is that he came not to be served but to serve.

PRAYER: Father, our sins deserved death but your Son, who was without sin, experienced death so that we might live. We would have no hope if you treated us as we deserved.

## Sunday Week 10

662-664

Jesus lifted up on the cross and in the Ascension into heaven

The Messiah's kingdom has begun

2816-2821

The kingdom of God has been coming since the Last Supper
  and will come in glory

The age of the outpouring of the Holy Spirit

Vocation to eternal life reinforces the duty to serve justice
  and peace in the world

The kingdom of God has begun in our midst in the coming of Christ. His kingdom comes differently than the kingdoms of this world—by humble servant love rather than by domination.

PRAYER: Christ our King, thy kingdom come. We love your reign and we long for its glorious completion.

## Monday Week 10

659-661

He ascended into heaven and is seated at the right hand of
  the Father

Christ appeared to the disciples after he rose from the dead

Christ opens heaven for mankind

1084-1085

Christ ascended into heaven now acts through the sacraments

Christ was present to humanity in one way during his life on earth. He is still present to us today through the sacraments of the Church. He himself still speaks God's Word to us through the Scriptures proclaimed in the Church; still imparts new life whenever anyone is baptized; still fully shares his death and new life in the Eucharist.

PRAYER: Lord Jesus, you are glorified at the Father's right hand. You have promised to be with us till the end of time. We give you thanks with all our hearts.

---

## Tuesday Week 10

---

571-573
Salvation accomplished once for all by the death of Christ
Christ suffered to enter his glory

613-617
By one man's obedience many will be made righteous
Christ loved us to the end
Christ's divinity and humanity make possible his redemptive
   sacrifice

We can have almost contradictory feelings about Christ's death on the cross. On the one hand, it seems an unthinkable horror that the Son of God would be put to death by mankind. But on the other hand, we feel an enormous gratitude to him for the love that led him to lay down his life that we might live.

PRAYER: Lord, you have treated us so bountifully. Your mercy is so great that we give our lives to you in complete trust.

**557-560**

Jesus went up to Jerusalem to die there, like the prophets

Palm Sunday: The messianic entrance into Jerusalem

**671-674**

Christ's reign in the Church is under attack by evil

The Church in travail prays, "Come, Lord Jesus"

Christ's second coming in glory is imminent

The kingdom of God has begun its reign in our midst even though its fullness is yet to be realized. We already see it, yet we know that its complete manifestation will be even greater.

PRAYER: Come, Lord Jesus. Your Church waits for you like a bride for the groom. Come quickly, Lord Jesus.

**554-556**

The Transfiguration: disclosure of Jesus' divine glory and prediction of the cross

He will change our lowly bodies to be like his glorious body

**668**

Christ's ascension signifies the participation of his humanity in God's power and authority

Jesus Christ is Lord: the Father has put all things under Christ's authority

Christ's glory has usually been hidden from the eyes of his followers and enemies alike. When his glory was briefly revealed on the mount, it was clear that no human being could oppose him. Yet it was not this display of power that would save us, but his humble obedience in the face of death. This is what Jesus discussed with Moses and Elijah on the mount.

PRAYER: Lord, we see your glory on the cross. May we also come to see your glory in heaven.

---

## Friday Week 10

631-635

Christ "descended into hell": he stayed in the realms of the dead prior to his resurrection

Christ went to the realms of the dead to release the just who had preceded him there

Christ's death destroyed the devil and delivered us from the fear of death

Jesus Christ, though he was God, was fully man. As a man, he tasted death just as all of us must. But his death, unlike that of any other human being, restored life to mankind. Just as he encountered others when he lived on earth, he also encountered the dead when he "descended into hell."

PRAYER: Lord Jesus Christ, we keep our eyes focused on you in life and in death. Bless us abundantly that we may live in you.

636-637
"He descended into hell"

656-658
Christ's resurrection, a historical event; the empty tomb
Christ, firstborn from the dead

665-667
Christ's ascension into heaven
Our hope of being with Christ in heaven

When Christ died, death was no longer the last word. Now his death sets free those held in bondage. Now our hope is that the evil of death will be a doorway for us into an eternal life with God.

PRAYER: Lord Jesus Christ, death could not hold you who are the Author of Life. We believe that you now intercede for us in the presence of the Father, and we trust in your unfailing care for us.

## Sunday Week 11

1373-1381

Christ now present to us in his Word, in the Church, in the poor and needy, and especially in the Eucharist

Transubstantiation: the conversion of the bread and wine into Christ's body and blood

Veneration of Christ present in the Eucharistic species

The tabernacle, place of reservation of the Eucharist: Christ remains mysteriously in our midst

The Real Presence of Christ in the Eucharist has been the subject of many conflicts among Christians. Some have maintained that the Eucharist is only a symbol of Christ's presence. But as the *Catechism* teaches, the Church believes Christ is "truly, really, and substantially" present in the Eucharist.

PRAYER: Lord, we bow before you. May all people come to you and humbly worship in your presence.

## Monday Week 11

1322-1327

The Eucharist completes Christian initiation

Christ perpetuates his sacrifice through the Eucharist

The Eucharist is the source and summit of the Christian life

2637-2643

Giving thanks in all things

Prayers of praise

The Eucharist is a celebration of praise and thanksgiving, uniting these two most important forms of prayer. It is the Holy Spirit himself who moves our hearts to praise God for who he is and to thank him for all his blessings.

PRAYER: Lord, you give us an abundance to meet our needs. We find great joy in the life you give us in the Eucharist.

---

## Tuesday Week 11

**1341-1344**
"Do this in memory of me"
Early Christians gathered on Sunday to celebrate the Eucharist

**2177-2179**
Obligation to attend Sunday Mass
Other holy days of obligation
Parish: a definite community with a pastor under the authority of a diocesan bishop

As Jesus gathered with the apostles at the Last Supper, so have his followers gathered with him around the world ever since, so that now the sun never sets on the celebration of the Eucharist.

PRAYER: The earth is full of your presence, Lord. You walk with us and invite us to your table, until we come to your eternal banquet. How good you are to us.

1345-1347

The basic order of the Eucharist: established from the earliest days of the Church

The two parts of the Mass forming one act of worship: Liturgy of the Word and Liturgy of the Eucharist

2180-2183

Sunday Mass obligation is excused for a serious reason

Deliberate failure to attend is a grave sin

Each baptized Christian has the right to attend the Eucharist. With the right there also comes duty, which the Church stipulates as fulfilled by attendance at Mass each Sunday. For those Christians who are able, it can also be a great practice of piety to attend the Eucharist on at least one additional day of the week.

PRAYER: Lord, I rejoice to hear your call to come to your banquet. Nothing else in my life is more important to me. Blessed be the God who does such marvelous things.

1356-1361

The Lord Jesus commanded us to celebrate the Eucharist

Eucharist: Thanksgiving, sacrifice, presence of Christ

The Real Presence: the bread and wine become the Body and Blood of Christ

1402-1405

Eucharist: pledge of the glory to come

Christ is now in heaven at the Father's right hand. Yet Christ is also present in this world through his Church, through her sacraments, and especially in the Eucharist. We do not yet see his full glory, but in the Eucharist we enter into it even now.

PRAYER: Come, Lord Jesus. We prepare for you by living holy lives. Come and bring us into the fullness of your glory.

## Friday Week 11

1396-1401
The Eucharist unites us with Christ
The Eucharist commits us to the poor
The state of our union with the Eastern Churches, and with the ecclesial communities of the Reformation
When intercommunion is permitted

2790
"Our Father"—communion of all Christians with one and the same Father

The current state of separation of Christians does not give the proper testimony to Christ and to his universal love of mankind. Yet in our times we have experienced the action of the Holy Spirit drawing us back toward each other, back toward our oneness in Christ.

PRAYER: Come, Holy Spirit. Show us the way to cooperate with you in restoring the unity of all disciples of Christ.

1406-1419
The Eucharist, heart and summit of the Church's life
Christ himself offers the sacrifice
Consecration and transubstantiation
Obligation to receive Communion once a year
Eucharistic adoration

To approach the sacrament of the Eucharist is to approach both the person of Christ and all he has achieved for the salvation of humanity. He told us that he gave himself for the life of the world, and he promised that by eating this bread we will live forever. There is no greater gift on the face of the earth.

PRAYER: Lord Jesus Christ, you are always present to us in the sacrament of the Eucharist, offering yourself to the Father on our behalf. Give us the grace to always see you present here and to participate worthily in your sacrifice.

**1382-1390**

Unity of sacrifice and Communion: the Lord's altar and the Lord's table

Preparing to receive Holy Communion

The Church's requirement of fasting before Communion

If properly disposed, receive Communion at each Mass

Receiving Communion is an integral part of Mass. However, it is necessary to be fully prepared: to be without mortal sin, to fast an hour ahead of time, to be attentive and reverential. Receiving the Eucharist in an unworthy manner is of no benefit. Receiving it worthily is of infinite benefit.

PRAYER: Lord, we fall so easily, but you have sought us out. You feed us with the finest wheat, your own Body and Blood, and you restore our souls.

**1913-1917**

Personal responsibility

Citizens should take an active part in public life

Fraud and subterfuge are wrong

Authorities need to inspire members of society to participate

**2196**

Love your neighbor as yourself

The presence of our neighbors in society is a constant call to love, a constant opportunity to serve others. The love of the Trinity for each other is the model guiding our love for each other in society.

PRAYER: Lord, your glory is revealed as your followers love one another and their fellow men and women. Help us to walk in your ways and to reflect your love in this world.

## Tuesday Week 12

1897-1900
Authority is necessary in human society
The role of authority to ensure the common good
Authority derives from God, and we have a duty to obey it

2234-2237
Fourth commandment: to honor all who have authority
Political authorities are to respect the rights of each person

The temptation for those in power is to use their position for their own gain. However, in God's plan, authority is a way to serve others, and the work of overseeing society for the common good of all is a noble charge.

PRAYER: Jesus, you said anyone who would be great must be last of all and servant of all. We need your grace to live this way in imitation of you.

## Wednesday Week 12

1901-1904
God established authority and thus authority does not derive its legitimacy from itself
The choice of political regime is up to citizens

Unjust and immoral laws are not binding in conscience

2238-2240
Moral obligations to pay taxes, vote, and defend one's country

God has a plan for political authority among men on earth. Those who are given political authority are stewards of what belongs to God, and they will have to give an account of their stewardship to their Master.

PRAYER: O God, guide the leaders of our country to set a direction of peace and justice. Give them the wisdom they need for their many duties.

## Thursday Week 12

1905-1909
The good of each individual is related to the common good
Common good: sum total of social conditions that allow
groups and individuals to reach their fulfillment

2241-2243
Prosperous nations are obliged to welcome foreigners
Duty not to follow civil authorities when they demand some-
thing contrary to the moral order
Conditions that justify armed resistance to oppression

The realities of society are incredibly complex and call for the utmost wisdom on the part of those who govern. Government needs to establish the common good and to have the wisdom and courage to overcome all forces acting against it.

PRAYER: Lord, you are the God of justice and peace. Give us peace, that each person may grow to his or her fulfillment in your plan.

## Friday Week 12

**1910-1912**
Human interdependence is increasing in the world
Universal common good of the human family

**2244-2246**
Different visions of man and his destiny behind different human institutions
The Church encourages political freedom and responsibility
The Church's mission in relation to politics

Modern progress makes this task of political leadership all the more urgent, since our new technologies are capable of so much good or evil. In this situation, the Church's wisdom is a source of guidance for shaping our political decisions.

PRAYER: Lord, give us wisdom to build society in peace and justice. If you were not upholding us we would surely fail.

## Saturday Week 12

**1918-1927**
All authority is from God
Human communities need authority
Authority is for the common good

Authority is not the invention of human beings but of God. This does not mean that those in authority may do whatever they please. Rather, they are called to diligently seek God's wisdom for establishing peace and justice.

PRAYER: Father, we are blessed to know your forgiveness for our many failings. Especially guide us to rightly carry out any duties of authority you have conferred upon us.

**407-409**
The overall sinful condition of the world
Ignorance of man's wounded nature gives rise to serious errors in various areas of life

**1886-1889**
Society is essential to the fulfillment of the human vocation
Priority of inner conversion of the heart for improving society
Charity: greatest social commandment

Mankind's sinful condition makes this a world of struggle and suffering. Yet, by God's grace, how many times in history have men, women, and societies risen above the tendency toward evil, and by charity attained achievements of great beauty and goodness! The struggle for justice and truth is hard but worth it.

PRAYER: Father, though we live and work under the shadow of troubles and trials, you preserve our lives. Deliver us from evil and allow us to serve you faithfully.

## Monday Week 13

**1881-1885**
The human person is central to every social organization
The principle of subsidiarity; limits of the state's intervention

**2312-2317**
Permanent validity of moral law, even during war
Modern warfare's pattern of widespread indiscriminate destruction
The arms race

Gathering individual men and women into society brings both benefits and dangers. Chief among the dangers is the possibility of war between tribes or nations. This combination of benefits and dangers will remain until the end of time. No social utopia will finally deliver mankind before Christ comes again.

PRAYER: Lord, guide those who govern society to be men and women of peace. Give them wisdom to be able to build up the common good.

## Tuesday Week 13

1877-1880
Humanity's vocation: to show forth the image of God
Relations of truth and love among men and women

2307-2311
All are obliged to work to avoid war
Lawful self-defense: just war
The duty to aid in national defense
Conscientious objectors

War is filled with horrors. It is the antithesis of relations of truth and love and the worst offense against the image of God that we bear. The vocation of civic leadership carries heavy duties of guiding society in its vocation of reflecting the relations of the Trinity.

PRAYER: Lord, teach us your ways of peace. May your kingdom come, your will be done, on earth as it is in heaven.

# Wednesday Week 13

849-856

Mission: a requirement of the Church's catholicity—God
wants all to be saved
The origin of the Church's mission is the love of the Trinity
The Holy Spirit is the agent of the Church's mission
For her mission, the Church shares the same earthly lot as
the world

The Church is necessarily missionary because Christ was
sent by the Father's love for all mankind. Until all mankind is
fully one in him, the Church presses on, calling all to come to
the love of Christ. The tasks are enormous, especially as we
try to bring Christ to new cultures throughout the world.

PRAYER: Father, we labor for you whether the work is easy
or hard, visibly successful or unsuccessful. We ask for your
help, assured of the grace we need for the mission you give
us.

# Thursday Week 13

709-710
Israel's Exile and the Remnant that returned

839-845
The Church's link with the Jewish people, the first to hear
the Word of God
With Christians, Muslims acknowledge the one merciful
Creator, the faith of Abraham, and the final judgment

Other religions prepare for the Gospel

Now we are faced with a diversity of religions that both conflict with each other and share some things in common. Christ is the only one who can unite them all. In him is the fullness of truth, which can satisfy the aspirations of all mankind to return to God.

PRAYER: Christ, you guide the course of history until all will be offered to the Father through you. We praise and glorify you for your mighty and wonderful deeds.

---

## Friday Week 13

---

80-83
Scripture and Tradition flow from the same divine wellspring
Tradition transmits the entirety of the Word of God

1200-1203
Liturgical diversity and unity of the mystery
All recognized liturgical rites are equal in dignity

Only in Christ can the diversity of the human race be reconciled. As his Word is preached throughout history, he unifies its expression in different ages. And as his worship spreads throughout the world, it also remains one.

PRAYER: Lord Jesus Christ, open my heart by your Holy Spirit. I want to know you, and love you, and serve you alone.

1890-1896
Development of the person in society
Subsidiarity
Reform of society according to the gospel

1207-1209
Unity of the diverse liturgical traditions in different cultures

In the Gospel of John, Jesus prays "that they may all be one ... even as you, Father, are in me, and I in you" (17:21-22). He calls for such a profound relationship among human beings that it is like the unity of the three divine Persons of the Trinity. This gives the greatest possible urgency to the need to transform society.

PRAYER: Father, you call all your children to treat each other with justice and love. Guide us to live according to your wisdom.

31-35
Ways of coming to know God
Proofs for the existence of God

54-55
God makes himself known
God gives evidence of himself in creation
Even after the Fall God continued to show his care for the human race

We find ourselves in a world of awesome beauty and order. The more we study the universe, the more amazing it appears to be. And the work and relationships of human beings manifest an awesome diversity—from great achievements of art, science, economics, technology, and social life. All these realities converge, convincing us that there is someone behind it all.

PRAYER: Thank you, Lord, for the goodness of life and creation. Help me to find you in the midst of it all.

*Monday Week 14*

36-38
Man's ability to know God with certainty
The difficulties in coming to know God by reason alone
Our need for God's revelation

**50-53**

God freely reveals himself and communicates his divine life
God reveals through deeds and words

Without revelation mankind is like a person in a dark room, unable to fully understand his surroundings. If a light is turned on, suddenly everything in the room makes sense. God's revelation is like that light, interpreting what would otherwise be completely confusing.

PRAYER: Father, thank you for bringing me out of darkness into your marvelous light.

---

## Tuesday Week 14

---

**56-58**

God's relationship to the nations: covenant with Noah
The perverse ambition to forge unity apart from God
Division into many nations limits the pride of fallen humanity
Great Gentiles of the Bible: Abel, Melchizedek, Noah, Daniel, Job

**2566-2569**

Man retains a desire for God and searches for him
God continues to call men and women to encounter him in prayer

The Fall is manifest socially in this world by the many divisions in the human race. In pride we went our own way, losing the ability to harmonize our lives with one another. It is remarkable that God still reached out to every person and that many "walked with God."

PRAYER: Father, I have heard your call throughout my life. Many times I have gone my own way. Please do not abandon me, but help me to turn to you always.

## Wednesday Week 14

62-64

The Exodus from Egypt and the covenant of Mount Sinai
Giving of the law through Moses and hope of salvation promised by the prophets
Holy women of God

2574-2577

Intercessory prayer
Moses' continual prayer as an intercessor for others who 'stands in the breach' for them

It is God who takes the initiative to form individuals as he formed Moses, and to form peoples as he formed Israel. He still calls us to be his coworkers today.

PRAYER: Father in heaven, how wonderful is your name throughout the earth. May all come to know you as Moses did, as Israel did, and as the Church does.

## Thursday Week 14

74-79

Christ commanded the apostles to preach the gospel to the entire world
Gospel handed on orally and in writing
Apostolic succession; Tradition

God's self-communication to mankind remains present and
active in the Church

Vatican II called the Church "the universal sacrament"
because it continues to make visible in the world what Christ
revealed about God. Christ set apart the apostles to continue
to testify to what he revealed. As the apostles added others to
their group, it expanded throughout the world. It continues
as one unified group today. In this way the Church has maintained the tradition Christ gave her.

PRAYER: Christ, you are no longer physically visible as you
were for Thomas to remove his doubts, but the testimony of
all your witnesses remains in the Church. Lord, I believe.

---

## Friday Week 14

---

88-95
Hierarchy of truths
*Sensus fidei*: the whole Church cannot err in belief
The faith once for all delivered to the Church
The Church's understanding of the realities and words of
    faith grows
Tradition, Scripture, and Magisterium stand together

Great peoples and civilizations come and go throughout
history, but the heritage of Christ is different. In the Church all
that Christ revealed remains: Christ the same yesterday, today,
and forever. However, the Church's understanding of Christ
and his revelation continues to develop throughout history.

PRAYER: Lord, guide us in facing the challenges of our day.
May your truth be honored throughout the world.

68-73

God reveals himself to mankind through Adam and Eve, Noah, Abraham, Moses, the prophets—and through his Son

96-100

Christ's revelation to the apostles
Tradition and Scripture
The sense of faith of the People of God
The Magisterium

We sense that the truth will set us free; the hope of finding it dominates our lives. In this context, God brings the truth to us, by revealing it to us in Christ, who is the Way, the Truth, and the Life. What he reveals will indeed set us free.

PRAYER: Lord, open our eyes to see all that you give us in Christ. Your Word is a greater treasure than silver and gold.

84-87

The Church as a whole always remains faithful to Christ

Magisterium: Authentic interpretation of the Word of God entrusted to the Church's teaching office

The Magisterium is a servant of the Word of God

1585-1586

The grace of ordination

Configuration to Christ as Priest, Teacher, and Pastor

The bishop receives grace to guide and defend the Church

Because of the Holy Spirit, both shepherd and flock within the Church faithfully receive the revelation of God in Christ. The whole Church always maintains the truth, not because of itself, but because of the work of the Holy Spirit.

PRAYER: Lord, bless the bishops you have called to serve you in the Church. May they have the strength and wisdom to represent you faithfully.

## Monday Week 15

282-289

Scientific studies about the origins of life

Permanence and universality of the question of origins

Other interpretations of the origins of man challenge Christianity

God reveals mankind's origin

Throughout history men and women have wondered about the origin and purpose of human life. They have come up with many stories to answer their questions. Each answer includes a view of where we came from and where we are going. God has revealed that we come from him and that our destiny is to share in his own life.

PRAYER: Father, we came forth from your hand and you lead us on to yourself. How great and mysterious is your plan.

## Tuesday Week 15

290-294
Creation is the common work of the Holy Trinity
The world depends on God, who created it for his glory
Holy Spirit, giver of life
God creates to communicate his love and goodness

The goal of human life is to glorify the Father of Jesus Christ. Everything else fits into that purpose. We even keep the commandments not for their own sake alone but in order to glorify God, the Author of our lives and of the commandments.

PRAYER: Father, have mercy on me, a sinner. May my life glorify you.

**295-298**
In wisdom and goodness God freely created the world
God creates out of nothing and gives life to the dead
New life for sinners

**992-996**
Resurrection of the body, by the power of the Creator
Christ's resurrection and our hope of resurrection

God, who created the world from nothing by his Word, is the same God who creates us anew in Christ and promises to raise us from the dead. God is our Creator from the beginning, now, and at the end—in creation, redemption, and resurrection.

PRAYER: Father, speak your Word and restore my heart. Come, Holy Spirit, and renew the face of the earth by your divine power.

**299-301**
Order and goodness in God's creation
The universe is destined for man, and man for God
God's presence to his creation, and his transcendence
God upholds and sustains creation

**2127-2128**
Agnosticism

The Church teaches that God can be known through his creation. Its order and goodness speak of its Creator, justifying the conclusion that there is indeed a God. But we are not left with simply a logical conclusion about God. He who is beyond all our reckoning has made himself present in our world. The agnostic, however, does not know whether to affirm this or not.

PRAYER: Lord God, thank you for testifying to yourself in creation and in revelation. I love you and your works with all my heart.

## Friday Week 15

309-314

Why does evil exist?

Freedom and preferential love mean angelic and human creatures can go astray

God is in no way the cause of moral evil

God derives good from evil

When we see God face to face we will know the reasons for his plan

Evil is a mystery. We experience it, but we do not have a satisfactory explanation for it. The innocent suffer, and at times those responsible for evil seem to go free. Why would God allow this? Later we will understand the answers to our questions, but already Christ has assured us that he has overcome evil.

PRAYER: Father, deliver us from evil. I thank you with all my heart for forgiving my sins; give me the grace to avoid offending you in the future.

315-324

God alone—Father, Son, and Holy Spirit—created the world
No creature can create from nothing
Creation: to show God's glory
God provides for all creatures
The mystery of evil

God is love, and his plan for creation is a plan of love. He wills nothing but good for us. Yet evil has entered our world through the temptation of God's enemy. We can only understand the condition of the human race if we understand these two sides of the story.

PRAYER: Great are your works, O God; they are established forever. You have shown us that we can trust in you to overcome all evil.

302-308

Creation in a state of journeying toward perfection
Divine providence: God cares for all
God's coworkers: we cooperate in God's plan
Dominion over the earth
God is at work in everything as its first cause

In one sense the creation is finished and in another sense it is not. This is true because God did not create the world to be a static finished product, like an artist's painting. Rather, he designed it to be in a process of development toward his ultimate plan. He calls human beings to be his coworkers in this process.

PRAYER: Lord, I embrace my responsibilities as part of your plan to bring this world to its fullness. Through all my joys and hardships I am working for you.

2402-2406

God entrusted the earth and its resources to the common stewardship of all mankind
The right to private property
Political authority has the right and duty to regulate the rights of ownership for the common good

2538-2540

The tenth commandment requires that we banish envy from our hearts

Until the end of time we will experience an unequal distribution of the goods of this world. Some of the inequality is legitimate, but some of it is unjust. While God gives us the right to own and use property, we must use it not only for our own good but also for the good of others.

PRAYER: Lord, you put mankind over all your creation and its resources. Grant that we may use everything for your honor and glory.

---

## Tuesday Week 16

---

### 2419-2425

It is morally unacceptable to make profit the exclusive end and norm of economic activity

The Church rejects totalitarian atheistic socialism

The Church rejects a capitalism that puts the marketplace before human labor

Centralized economic planning perverts social bonds

Reasonable regulation of the marketplace is to be commended

The Church teaches us how to justly and prudently care for others in our social and economic lives. The Church's teaching, based on the gospel, sheds a unique light on human interactions in all areas of life.

PRAYER: Lord, may your kingdom come among us. Your ways are the ways of truth and life. By them we live.

**2427-2429**
Work is a duty
Bringing the spirit of Christ into our work

**2828-2830**
Give us this day our daily bread

**2433**
Access to employment without discrimination

**2435-2436**
When strikes are acceptable and when they are not
Social security contributions and unemployment

Normally we gain what we need for life by our work. Yet it is still appropriate to be grateful to God because both creation's resources and our ability to work are sustained by his divine power.

PRAYER: Lord, help me to accept the hardships of work and to use the gifts you have given me to make a contribution to society.

**2430-2432**
Principal task of the state: to guarantee security so that those who work can benefit from their labor
Businesses are responsible to society for their economic and ecological impact
Profits, necessary but not the only goal

## 2415-2418

Our dominion over creation is limited by the quality of life of
our neighbors and of future generations

Issues in the use and care of animals

If we misuse creation we steal from other men and women
what is rightfully theirs, for the rights we have to use creation
are shared with others who have the same rights. We are to
be stewards of creation so that its God-given resources are a
blessing for all.

PRAYER: Father, your divine goodness is seen in what you
have made. You provide abundantly for us.

---

## Friday Week 16

---

## 2434

Justice in wages

## 2410-2414

The importance of living up to promises and contracts

Justice: commutative, legal, distributive

When gambling is acceptable and when it is not

The sin of slavery

## 2426

Economic development and growth in production

God's intention for our use of property is that we might
develop as persons in his image and likeness. In our attempts
to fulfill his intention, we confront many issues concerning the
proper distribution and use of property at all levels of society.

PRAYER: Lord, give me wisdom for all the decisions of my life; and guide us as a society to ways of justice for all men and women.

---

## Saturday Week 16

---

2450-2463
Seventh commandment, against stealing
The right to private property for all men and women
Moral law forbids slavery
Stewardship of creation
Giving alms to the poor

The commandment against stealing stems from the right to own property, a right given by God to all men and women. Depriving others of their rightful property deprives them of the very means of life, which they need for themselves and their families. Far from stealing, each person is called to work so that he has enough to support himself and to give to others who are in need (see Eph 4:28).

PRAYER: Lord, give us all we need for our lives, for we know it comes from you. Give us wisdom to care for the things of this world.

**2407**
Solidarity with our neighbor

**2437-2442**
Inequalities in resources create economic gaps between
nations
Rich nations have a grave moral responsibility toward other
nations unable to secure their own development
It is the role of the laity, and not of the Church's pastors,
to directly intervene in political and social structures

Each person has a great influence on the good of society and of a great number of other persons. Thus, a sense
of solidarity with our fellow men and women is absolutely
necessary for the successful organization of social life.
Without it we emphasize what is good for ourselves while
we neglect the needs of others.

PRAYER: Lord Jesus, you told us to love our neighbor as
ourselves. You were the model of such love without limits.
Pour out your Spirit of love within our hearts.

## Monday Week 17

**2401**
Justice and charity in the care of earthly goods and the fruits
of labor

**2408-2409**
The seventh commandment forbids theft
Obvious and urgent necessity may permit taking goods of
others to meet essential needs

2534-2537

The tenth commandment forbids greed, avarice, and coveting the goods of others

In God's plan, people need to be able to use the earthly things to maintain and develop their lives. We violate others if we take unjustly what is theirs.

PRAYER: Lord, give me your heart of justice. I want to praise you in purity of heart, free of sin.

## Tuesday Week 17

541-546

"The kingdom of God is at hand"
The Father's will: to share his divine life with us by gathering us to his Son Jesus Christ in the Church
Everyone is called to enter the kingdom
The kingdom belongs to the poor and lowly
Jesus shares the life of the poor and invites sinners to his table

Jesus came into a world where every man and woman seems to want to rule their own world. He lived a new way, not seeking his own glory but the glory of the One who sent him. He put the kingdom of God absolutely first.

PRAYER: Jesus, you bring us the pearl of great price. Give us the grace to sell everything else to attain it.

**1928-1933**

The person is the ultimate end of society and has rights prior to society

If it does not respect rights, authority can rely only on violence

The duty of being a neighbor is more urgent toward the disadvantaged

Christ's command to love our enemies

**2268-2269**

The fifth commandment forbids both direct and indirect murder

God forbids the taking of another person's life. In fact, he goes so far as to command that we love our enemies. This does not mean we must condone anyone's evil behavior, but it does show that all persons have equal dignity before God.

PRAYER: Lord, have mercy on us for all our offenses against our neighbors. Come to the aid of the weak and help us be instruments of your peace.

**1934-1938**

By God's plan, abilities and resources are not distributed equally among men

Some inequalities are sinful

*"I should Pray as if everything depended on God and work as if everything depended on me."*

**2831-2834**
The drama of hunger in the world
Establishing justice on earth
Sharing material and spiritual goods out of love for others

The differences between individual men and women, rather than the similarities, are usually most striking to us. Yet the dignity of each person as a creature of God is more important than any differences between individuals. Each person is willed by God and will exist forever, while all the treasures of creation will pass away.

PRAYER: Lord, you know the hearts of all mankind and you judge each one justly. Open our hearts to serve our brothers and sisters without malice or discrimination.

---

## Friday Week 17

---

**1939-1942**
Solidarity displayed in distribution of goods and remuneration for work
Efforts for a more just society
The Church's historic record of social charity

**2302-2306**
Safeguarding peace
Anger, the desire for revenge
Hatred, wishing another evil

Lack of peace between individuals and nations is the source of the gravest suffering among men and women.

Peace is so important that Christ said, "Blessed are the peace-makers." Peace can be established only when men and women display active charity for one another.

PRAYER: Lord Jesus Christ, you established peace between God and man. May your peace now spread to all men and women. Lord, make me an instrument of your peace.

---

## Saturday Week 17

1943-1948
Social justice and solidarity
The rights that come from the dignity of the person
Equality of and differences between persons

2551-2557
Tenth commandment: forbidding avarice and envy
Detachment from riches; thirst for God

Jesus' parable of the seed that fell among thorns speaks of our involvement with the riches of this world, choking off the life of God within us. This does not mean that the things God created are evil. Rather, it means that when we dedicate our time and efforts to simply building up our own earthly wealth, we lose the spiritual treasures of a life of love and service to God and others.

PRAYER: Lord Jesus, preserve me from temptations to envy those who grow rich in this world. I know the only wealth that will follow me into your presence will be what comes from obeying and following you.

8-6-00

2052-2055
"What must I do to have eternal life?"
If you would enter life keep the commandments
Evangelical counsels of poverty, chastity, and obedience

1038-1041
The Last Judgment, followed by eternal life or eternal pun-
  ishment
Only the Father knows when Christ will come again

In two commandments Christ summarizes the duties to
God on which we will be judged: love of God above all else,
and love of our neighbor as ourselves. In practice we can
understand what we love by considering what we will sacrifice. Do we sacrifice time and resources for God? For others?

PRAYER: Christ, when you come again I pray that you will
find me faithful. Give me the grace to sacrifice everything else
in order to follow you.

## Monday Week 18

2058-2063
God's law reveals his glory
God gave the commandments only after he first showed his
  love for his people

1776-1778
Conscience is the voice of a law of which man knows he is
  not the author

Conscience guides us to do good and avoid evil

God's laws are not arbitrary tests of an uncaring sovereign. No, God created us for happiness with each other and with himself, and his commandments are the ways of happiness that fit our nature.

PRAYER: Father, blessed are those who love your ways. Give me the grace to steadfastly honor and keep your statutes.

## Tuesday Week 18

2064-2069
The Ten Commandments state what is required for love of
   God and neighbor
Observance of the Ten Commandments is required of all

1965-1968
The New Law expressed in the Sermon on the Mount
The Holy Spirit writes the New Law on our hearts
Imitating the perfection of the heavenly Father

The teaching of Christ has an entirely new quality that liberates those who hear it in faith. It is in one sense more demanding than the Old Law, yet it is also freeing. Through it, Christ calls us to imitate the perfection of our heavenly Father.

PRAYER: O Lord, let your steadfast love come to me, with the fulfillment of all your promises. As your child I want to please you.

2070-2074

Ten Commandments: the fundamental duties and rights
  inherent in the nature of the person
The Ten Commandments reveal grave obligations to God
  and fellow man, and are unchangeable
Holiness of life from union with Christ

1969-1972

Christ's new command to love others as he loved us
The apostles developed our understanding of Christ's teaching

The New Law is a law of love, grace, and freedom. How
dark life would be without the Law of God and the teaching
of Christ. God came to reveal his ways to us—like a light
shining in a dark place. With his law we begin to see the
meaning of life and we begin to lift our lives to him.

PRAYER: Lord, you said that hearing and obeying your
Word is like building on rock. I want to build on you as my
sure foundation.

1961-1964

God chose Israel to be his people and revealed his Law to
  them
The Law does not give us the strength to fulfill it
The Law has a special function of disclosing sin
The Old Law prepares for the gospel

**2056-2057**
The Decalogue: "ten words" written "with the finger of God"

The Ten Commandments contain truths that could have been established by human reason. However, the fact that God revealed the commandments establishes his will beyond debate. Therefore, this revelation has been the basis of all teaching of morality.

PRAYER: Lord, you created us, and you created all of our abilities. Help us use our abilities to learn and follow your commands.

---

## Friday Week 18

---

**396**
Original sin: freedom put to the test

**1954-1960**
Natural Moral Law written in the soul of every person
Natural Law, valid in all cultures and in all periods of history
Manmade laws need to be consistent with Natural Law

God created this world in a way that reflected his own goodness and reliability. Thus, when we come into the world we find it already to be a place with a certain order that is given by God and that we may not violate without offending God, others, and even the truth of our own being.

PRAYER: Father, the heavens and the earth display your love and power at work. Help us to understand your will for us and for our world and to live according to it.

1975-1986
God's Law is a fatherly instruction
Christ is the end of the Law
Natural Law expresses the dignity of the human person and is unchangeable
The Old Law is summed up in the Ten Commandments, and prepares for the gospel
The New Law

The love of God's Law is profoundly expressed in the Old Testament (for example, in Psalm 119). Such love would be unthinkable if the law were not perfectly good for us. It is an expression of a loving Father who wants to bless our lives abundantly.

PRAYER: Lord God, your Word is a lamp to my feet and a light to my path. Teach me all your ordinances.

142-149
Revelation: God addresses us to bring us into a relationship with himself
Abraham: father of all who believe
Faith: assurance of things hoped for, conviction of things not seen
Mary: perfect embodiment of faith

The most important truths are known only by faith: that God exists and that he loves and welcomes us in Christ. By faith we know these truths more certainly than we know anything else, and we know that God will never fail us or forsake us.

PRAYER: All-loving God, I believe what you have revealed in Christ. I entrust my life to you.

---

*Monday Week 19*

---

150-152
Faith: adherence to God and assent to all he reveals
Believing in God is believing in Christ, whom he sent
The Holy Spirit's role in our faith

197, including the Creeds
Embrace the Creed with faith, and enter into communion with God and with the Church

By faith we come into a relationship with God. The mystery of God is beyond our full comprehension, but when we accept it in faith we enter into a communion with the Father, the Son, and the Holy Spirit, and with all other believers.

PRAYER: I believe in God the Father almighty, Creator of heaven and earth. I believe in Jesus Christ, his only Son, our Lord. He was conceived by the power of the Holy Spirit and born of the Virgin Mary. He suffered under Pontius Pilate, was crucified, died, and was buried. He descended to the dead. On the third day he rose again. He ascended into heaven and is seated at the right hand of the Father. He will come again to judge the living and the dead. I believe in the Holy Spirit, the holy catholic Church, the communion of saints, the forgiveness of sins, the resurrection of the body, and life everlasting. Amen

---

## Tuesday Week 19

---

153-159
Faith is a gift of God
Faith is a human act, not contrary to reason
External proofs of the faith: miracles, prophecies, the holiness of the Church
Faith is certain, but seeks understanding
Relationship of faith and science

Christ said a mustard seed of faith was enough; any "yes" to God, no matter how small, is an act of trust in God and in his truth.

PRAYER: Father, thank you for the gift of faith. Thank you for the new life you give us through faith. I entrust my life to you.

160-162
Faith is a free response to God
Faith is necessary for salvation

1257-1261
Baptism is necessary for salvation
Baptism of blood; baptism of desire
The death of unbaptized children

God wants our free adherence to him. He gives us the grace to seek him and to accept his initiatives of love for us. Those who believe and are baptized come to life and salvation in Christ.

PRAYER: Come, Holy Spirit, help me to persevere in the faith the Father has given me. I believe; help my unbelief.

163-165
Faith, the beginning of eternal life
We walk by faith, not by sight
We perceive God only in part

1020
Death: entrance into everlasting life
The prayer of the Church at the moment of going home to heaven

In heaven we shall see God face to face, as he is. Faith gives us a beginning taste of heaven even now. We benefit from the great example of those men and women of faith who have gone before us. They lived with their eyes on the unseen glory of Christ, visible now only by faith.

PRAYER: Father, thank you for the faith of my parents and others who taught me the truth about you. Allow me to be a witness of the faith to others.

## Friday Week 19

170-171
The language of faith: words in touch with spiritual realities
The Church guards the truths of faith and teaches them

857-860
The Church guards the deposit of faith received from the apostles
The apostles' successors: the college of bishops
Jesus was sent by the Father; the apostles were sent by Jesus

The apostles witnessed everything Jesus said and did from the time he began his public ministry until he ascended into heaven. They were set apart by Christ to be the ones who definitively proclaimed what they were shown by Christ. Their witness is still the foundation of the Church today.

PRAYER: O my God, you founded your Church through your son Jesus Christ for the sake of all who would believe. Bless the leaders of your Church so that they may continue their faithful witness to what you gave the Church.

176-184
Faith: assent to God's revelation of himself
Faith: a supernatural gift and a human act
Faith is necessary for salvation

By faith we commit ourselves to God. It is an act of trust, of saying yes to all that God has revealed, holding that he cannot deceive us. We can do this only by the grace of God. The Holy Spirit moves our heart and converts it.

PRAYER: Lord, blessed is the person who trusts in you. You alone protect and guide us at all times.

748-752
The light of Christ shines visibly from the Church
The Spirit has endowed the Church with holiness
Church: local community of Christians and universal community of believers

811-812
Christ makes his Church one, holy, catholic, and apostolic
We recognize the divine source of the Church by faith

Many conversions to Christ have come when people encounter holiness among Christians and in the liturgies of the Church. Though sin remains in the Church on earth, still there is something unique found here and nowhere else: the love, peace, and holiness wrought by the Holy Spirit among the followers of Christ.

PRAYER: Lord, I have not been an undivided witness to you throughout my life. Draw me nearer and nearer to you that I might reflect you to others.

## *Monday Week 20*

753-757
The Church: People of God and body of Christ
The Church: sheepfold, cultivated field, building of God, family of God, holy temple, and new Jerusalem

796
Christ, the Bridegroom; Church, the bride
Christ cares for the Church as for his own body

The Church is such a great reality that we can look at it in many different ways. Key to them all is the Church's relation to the Trinity. She is the People of God, the bride of Christ, the temple of the Holy Spirit.

PRAYER: How lovely is your dwelling place, O Lord of hosts! My soul longs, yea, faints for the courts of the Lord (Ps 84:1-2).

## Tuesday Week 20

758-762
The Church's origin, foundation, and mission
God's eternal plan to bring all the followers of his Son into one holy Church
The world was created for the sake of the Church
The reunification of all in the Church is God's response to the conflicts provoked by sin

At the end of time there will be only Christ and his bride, the Church. Our true identity is our identity as a member of the Church, which is Christ's body. In Christ's body we find not only our own destiny but also communion with all other believers in the life of God.

PRAYER: O God, you have blessed us abundantly by calling us to your Son Jesus Christ. We choose the way of fidelity to him in our whole lives.

**763-766**

The Church is the reign of Christ already present in mystery

The twelve apostles, with Peter as their head, are the foundation stones of the New Jerusalem

Church: born of Christ's total self-giving; born from his pierced heart

**792-795**

Christ is Head of his body, the Church, preeminent in everything

The oneness of all members of the Church with each other and with Christ their Head is a great mystery. It is possible because of the one Spirit dwelling in each, and because of the one Head over all who is Christ. We have already entered into this oneness, which we will see fully revealed at the end of time.

PRAYER: Lord, all the nations will turn to you. Where we now experience division you bring healing and life.

**772-773**

The Church's holiness is the communion of men with God

**830-835**

The Church is catholic because Christ is present in her and because Christ sent her to the whole human race

A "particular Church," or diocese, is catholic through its
communion with the Church of Rome
The rich variety within the Church worldwide shows its
catholicity

Divided humanity needs a source of union greater than
anything it possesses within itself. This source of union is the
life of God in Christ. Expressing the union that we have in
him requires all our abilities.

PRAYER: Lord, God of holiness, bring your presence into
our midst. We proclaim your name throughout the world,
saying, "Put your trust in him."

---

## Friday Week 20

---

172-175
One faith, one Lord, one baptism, one God and Father
The Church's one voice

813-816
Variety of God's gifts and diversity of recipients
Bond of charity
The Church of Christ subsists in the Catholic Church

The unity of the Church is visible and beyond any other
experience of unity on earth. The Real Presence of Christ,
dwelling in the Church and in her individual members by the
Holy Spirit, makes the Church a unique reality. Free human
beings come together as one in the Church because they are
all animated by the same Holy Spirit and are all under the
headship of the one Lord Jesus Christ.

PRAYER: Lord, help us to overcome every division that comes from our sins. Build your Church to be one with you and with the Father in heaven.

---

## Saturday Week 20

---

777-780
The Church:
  Assembly of those called together by God's Word
  Means and goal of God's plan
  Visible and spiritual
  Sacrament of salvation

866-870
The Church: one, holy, catholic, apostolic
The Church of Christ subsists in the Catholic Church

The Church as a living body on earth, filled with the Holy Spirit and hierarchically structured, mysteriously represents Christ in the midst of history. Christ is still present to mankind and to individual men and women through all the aspects of the Church: its sacraments, its ministers and members, its teaching, its holiness.

PRAYER: Lord Jesus Christ, you remain with us until the end of time. Open our eyes to see you, to hear you, and to follow you.

**1117-1121**

The sacraments make the Church and communicate the mystery of communion with God

Successors of the apostles act in Christ's name and person

**1272-1274**

In baptism we are incorporated in Christ

Indelible character of baptism

Baptism consecrates the Christian for worship

The great and fundamental change of baptism brings us out of the kingdom of darkness and into God's kingdom of light. All the baptized together make up the body of Christ, serving God as one in this world.

PRAYER: Father, you claimed me for your own through baptism. Help me to bring honor and glory to your name.

## Monday Week 21

**1122-1126**

The Church's mission to baptize is implied in her mission to evangelize

Sacraments: to sanctify men, to build up the body of Christ, to give worship to God

**1153-1155**

God's initiative and our response of faith

God's Word, integral to the sacraments

Sacraments make the wonders of God present

God speaks a Word to our hearts that has power to create us anew. He then draws us to respond to him in the sacraments, through which the change in our hearts is clearly and outwardly signified.

PRAYER: Father, may all men and women hear your Word and share your life.

## Tuesday Week 21

1086-1090
Apostles: sacramental signs of Christ
Apostolic succession
Christ is present in the Church, in the sacrifice of the Mass, and in all the sacraments

1135-1139
The whole Christ, Head and members, celebrate the liturgy as one
In the sacraments we participate in the eternal liturgy

When the saints go to heaven to join Christ, they worship the Father with him in the power of the Holy Spirit. If we could see heaven when we went to Mass, we would know that we are joining that great throng in a pleasing offering to God.

PRAYER: Holy, holy, holy, Lord God Almighty, heaven and earth are full of your glory.

## Wednesday Week 21

817-822
There have been rifts in the Church from its beginning
All the baptized are accepted as brothers by the Church
Many elements of truth are found outside the Church
Steps back to unity: renewal, conversion of heart, prayer in
common, fraternal knowledge, ecumenical formation, dialogue, collaboration

In the past century there has been a great desire among Christians to return to a visible unity as followers of Christ. Many misunderstandings still remain, and at times progress toward unity seems slow. However, the Holy Spirit is turning the hearts of Christians towards each other in spite of divisions that have existed for centuries.

PRAYER: Father, by your mercy, grant that we may find the paths to unity so that the world will know you through our Lord Jesus Christ.

## Thursday Week 21

166-169
Our faith is not isolated; we receive it from others and live it
with others.
The Church sustains our faith

874-875
Christ is the source of the Church's ministry
No one proclaims the gospel to himself

Ministers of grace act (in the person of Christ the Head)

The great mystery of the Church is a mystery of shared life in Christ. Our sisters and brothers in Christ are in a unique relationship with us because we sustain and build each other up in Christ by the grace and the responses in faith we share.

PRAYER: Lord, increase the faith of your Church. Bless us all with an ever clearer vision of all you have given us, with faithfulness to your call.

---

## Friday Week 21

781-782
We are saved not as individuals but as a unified people
The Old Covenant prepared the New Covenant
Distinctive marks of the People of God: born anew, sons of
    God, new commandment of love

2786-2787
Our Father: a new relationship with God

2759-2760
Our Father, the Lord's Prayer

It seems that many either disregard God or understand the world as something he created and then left on its own. But our race's obvious distance from God is not something he wants to leave as it is. Like a loving Father, he seeks out his lost children to bring them back to himself.

PRAYER: Teach us your ways, Father. You have been gracious to us according to your promise and your eternal love.

802-810

Christ redeemed us to be his own people

All are called to belong to God's one family

The Church: body of Christ, bride of Christ, temple of the Holy Spirit

The Church: a people of unity based on the unity of the Trinity

When time is over, when history is past, it is the Church that will remain. What we are then will be what we are as members of Christ's body. Then we will see that the meaning of our lives and of our actions is the meaning they have in Christ alone.

PRAYER: Lord Jesus, give us the grace to grow to full maturity in the way you plan for us. We want to be your faithful bride, giving glory to the Father.

551-553

Through his apostles, Jesus guides the Church

"I will give you the keys of the kingdom": authority to govern the house of God

880-882

The pastoral office of Peter and the apostles belongs to the Church's foundation and is continued by the bishops under the primacy of the Pope

Pope: source and foundation of the unity of the Church

Christ founded his Church not on ideas but on people, and specifically on the apostles gathered around Peter. From the earliest days until now, we find the Church ordered around the Bishop of Rome with his brother bishops throughout the world.

PRAYER: Lord, you shepherd us yourself through your Church. Strengthen the Pope and the bishops for their work of service.

861-862

The sacred order of bishops: enduring office of shepherding the Church

883-887

The college of bishops has authority over the Church but only when united with the Roman Pontiff

Ecumenical council: all the bishops gathered with the Pope
College of bishops: expression of variety and universality of
the People of God

Christ willed that certain men among his followers would lead and care for his flock. These are the bishops. Their exercise of authority differs from the exercise of authority in affairs that are strictly earthly. They in no way own the Church, for it belongs only to Christ.

PRAYER: Pray for your local bishop: Lord, grant every grace to Bishop _____ for the duties you have given him.

---

## Tuesday Week 22

2030-2034
The Christian fulfills his vocation in the Church
From the Church the Christian receives the Word of God,
the grace of the sacraments, and an example of holiness
Church: pillar and bulwark of truth
Magisterium: ordinary and universal

Men and women continually find new ways to resist God's truth. But in the midst of the world the Church clings to Christ's ways, challenging every falsehood. The Church faithfully offers every person a way to find the truth and to live out his or her God-given vocation.

PRAYER: Father, you never change. You are faithful and true. Thank you for the gift of your Church, reflecting your life in our midst.

2035-2040

The charism of infallibility

The Magisterium authoritatively presents the truth about humanity

The Holy Spirit can use anyone to enlighten others in Christ's truth: pastors, theologians, laity

Personal conscience should not be set in opposition to the moral law and the Magisterium of the Church

1779-1782

The ability to hear and follow our consciences

The person must not be forced to act contrary to his or her conscience

It is true that the person must follow his or her conscience, but there is also a duty to correctly form our consciences. The guidance of the Church is not meant to be an enemy of conscience but a help to find the truth and walk in it.

PRAYER: O God, you make me steadfast in your ways. Without you my weakness would be my undoing.

2041-2043

The Church requires certain practices on the part of the faithful in order to guarantee an indispensable minimum of prayer and moral effort

The five precepts of the Church

**2691**

The church is the proper place for liturgical prayer of the
    parish community
Choice of a proper place for personal prayer

All that the Church gives us is for our good. Even the laws
of the Church are meant to form us in the performance of
the basic requirements of life in Christ. For instance, Christ
requires all his followers to do acts of penance. The Church
specifies some acts of penance that we might at least mini-
mally fulfill Christ's command.

PRAYER: Lord, write your laws on our hearts that we might
be holy as you are.

---

## Friday Week 22

---

Between numbers 2051 and 2052

Three versions of the Ten Commandments—from the books
    of Exodus and Deuteronomy, and from a traditional cate-
    chetical version

Frequently God gives us information in order of importance. This is true of the Ten Commandments. The first commandments deal with our relationship with God, who comes
before all else. The rest of the commandments direct us in our
relationships with people. They forbid what is wrong, in order
of importance: Don't take your neighbor's life; don't take
your neighbor's spouse; don't take your neighbor's property;
don't take your neighbor's reputation; and don't even desire
to take those things secretly in your heart.

PRAYER: Father, thank you for your commandments, which give light to our fallen world. May the truth and justice of your will reign on earth.

---

## Saturday Week 22.

---

2047-2051
The moral life
The precepts of the Church
Magisterium and infallibility

2075-2082
Permanent validity of the Ten Commandments
God's commandments are part of his relationship with us
What God commands he makes possible by grace

God commands only what is good for us. While obedience may seem arduous at times, it is a lighter burden to live under his commands than to follow the ways of sin—which give fleeting pleasure and long-term suffering.

PRAYER: Lord, I love your Word. Your ways are a greater treasure to me than gold and silver. By your Word I find life.

**888-896**
Teaching office of bishops and priests
Magisterium: professing the true faith without error
Infallibility exercised by the Pope, and by the body of
    bishops together with the Pope
Sanctifying and governing office of bishops and priests
The Pope confirms and defends the authority of the bishops

The bishop and priests of each local diocese teach, sanctify,
and govern the People of God in the things of Christ. Their
office is a service to Christ and his disciples. Their positions
must not be misunderstood as claims to privilege and power
over others, but as a serious duty to serve them.

PRAYER: Lord, bless the Holy Father in his leadership of the
Church. Guide our bishops and priests to lead us as you
yourself would.

**897-900**
The laity's mission: to seek the kingdom of God by engaging
    in social, political, and economic affairs according to
    God's will
The apostolate of pastors cannot be totally effective without
    the apostolate of the laity

**2044-2046**
Christians build up the Church by the constancy of their
    convictions and the morality of their lives

Christians can hasten the coming of the reign of God

It is common to blame troubles in the Church on the bishops and priests, but the laity also have duties they may fail to perform. Each layperson must consider whether he or she has faithfully brought the spirit of the gospel into his or her social, political, and economic lives. God's kingdom depends on all, lay and ordained, carrying out their missions in all spheres of life.

PRAYER: Father, in Christ you have sent out a great army of witnesses to your kingdom of love. May we all be found faithful in your service.

## Tuesday Week 23

901-903
Laity, called and prepared to bear rich fruit
The laity consecrate the world to God
Parents' role in sanctifying

1546
All the faithful are consecrated to be a holy priesthood

A priest is a mediator between God and mankind. His work is to reach out to men and women in the name of God and to make offerings to God on their behalf. The one high priest who does all this is Christ, but all the members of his body share in it. The laity's part in his priesthood includes all their daily actions, which at one and the same time represent God to the world and offer the world to God.

PRAYER: Father, you sent your Son in the midst of this fallen world to bring it back to you. I accept your call to follow him. Help me to grow in his holiness.

---

## Wednesday Week 23

904-913

Lay participation in Christ's prophetic office by evangelization in the ordinary circumstances of life, by collaboration in catechetical formation, and by expressing opinions on matters pertaining to the good of the church

Lay participation in Christ's kingly office by overcoming sin, by ordering institutions and conditions of the world to the norms of justice and morality, and by cooperative service to the ecclesial community

Each baptized Catholic is associated with Christ and with the mission of his Church. The world has great need of the witness and service of all the laity so that souls may be eternally saved and so that the ways of life of society may reflect the truth and justice of God.

PRAYER: Here I am, Lord; send me to serve your purposes. Strengthen me and give me wisdom to help others know you, love you, and serve you.

---

## Thursday Week 23

914-921

Religious or consecrated life: poverty, chastity, and obedience

Hermits: stricter separation from the world for penance and prayer and for personal intimacy with Christ

1618-1620
Virginity for the sake of the kingdom: renouncing the good
  of marriage to follow the Lord
The Lord gives meaning to Matrimony and to virginity

From the earliest days of the Church, certain men and
women felt called by God to imitate Christ in a life of poverty,
celibacy, and strict obedience. Though not all Christians are
called to live this way, the Church recognizes this life, called
consecrated life, as a key part of the life of the Church.

PRAYER: Lord, you have never left us without a witness to
your holiness. In a special way you maintain that witness in
the holy lives of those who are consecrated for the religious
life.

---

## Friday Week 23

---

930-933
Societies of apostolic life
Spirit of the Beatitudes
Consecration: looking forward to Christ's coming

2544-2547
Poverty of heart, detachment from riches
Abandonment to God's providence

The poverty of detachment from earthly possessions is
necessary for every Christian. The vow of poverty of the consecrated religious life is not for everyone, however, but those
who are called to it live a life that expresses where all of us are
headed: to the kingdom of God, which will be fully manifest

when Christ returns. Poverty means having Christ as our true treasure.

PRAYER: Lord Jesus Christ, you are my treasure and my joy. Your kingdom is the pearl of great price for which I give up all else.

---

## Saturday Week 23

934-945
Christ sent the apostles to act in his person
St. Peter, visible foundation of the Church
Pope, bishops, priests, deacons, laity
Consecrated life

After his resurrection, Christ ascended to the right hand of the Father in heaven. From there he guides the life of each person and the course of human history, promising to the apostles, "I am with you always, to the close of the age" (Mt 28:20). Surely it was this promise that gave Peter the courage to accept the plan of God to build the Church on him.

PRAYER: Lord, we embrace every duty you give us, waiting for you in confidence. May your name be praised and honored.

770-771

Christ established his Church to communicate truth and grace to all

1179-1186

Where the liturgy is celebrated, there the faithful gather as the Church's living stones

Church building: house of prayer and of the Eucharist, with Christ present and active

Passing the threshold of the church: leaving the world of sin and entering the world of new life

Christ's Church is a unique reality—the People of God who remain fully human yet already share divine life. It is not the building but the people who are the Church. Yet church buildings are important for expressing the spiritual realities of God's people, who gather there in the sacramental presence of Christ.

PRAYER: Lord, you elevate our poor lives by associating them with your divine life. You are the God of the heavens, yet you are not ashamed to dwell with us.

## Monday Week 24

774-776

The sacraments spread the grace of Christ throughout the Church his body

The Church is the instrument Christ uses for the salvation of all

846-848

The Church is necessary for salvation

Those who through no fault of their own do not know Christ and his Church, yet seek him with a sincere heart, may also achieve eternal salvation

It is hard to imagine what the unity of all mankind will look like. However, we do know that unity will not be fully established until the end of time. Then we will see clearly that it is only in Christ, as his body, that we again become one as a human race.

PRAYER: Preserve us, O Lord, from the full implications of our sins. Take notice of us and care for us that we might grow into our full unity in you.

---

## Tuesday Week 24

---

836-838

In different ways Catholics, other believers, and all mankind are called to the unity of the People of God

Charity is necessary for salvation

1267-1271

Baptism incorporates us into the Church

The baptized person no longer belongs to himself but to Christ

A controversy arose several decades ago when an American priest began to teach that the doctrine that there is no salvation outside the Church meant that only formally recognized members of the Catholic Church could go to heaven. The Church excommunicated him, and he later recanted. Today's reading explains the authentic meaning of this teaching.

PRAYER: Lord, you are glorious in your Church. Open eyes, hearts, and minds to know you, to love you, and to find you within the Church.

---

## Wednesday Week 24

---

**1369-1372**

The entire Church is united with the offering and intercession of Christ

The role of the Pope and local bishop in every Eucharist

The saints in heaven and Christians in purgatory are also part of each Eucharist

**2822-2827**

"Love one another as I have loved you"

The union of all things in Christ

In Christ her Head, the Church has already accomplished God's perfect will. We are all one in him; we are all joined with him in his perfect sacrifice. In our daily lives we are to learn to imitate him and his obedience to the Father.

PRAYER: Lord Jesus, you are enthroned at the Father's right hand because you obeyed him even to the point of death. By the grace of your Spirit, we are ready to follow your example.

**2665-2669**

Christian prayer primarily addresses the Father, but it also addresses Jesus Christ

Simplest prayer: to call on the name of Jesus

**525-526**

The glory of the night of Christ's birth

Entering the kingdom by becoming children of God in Christ

So many forces in daily life pull us away from an awareness of God—forces both outside and within us. In the midst of these challenges, the simple practice of calling on the name of Jesus is a prayer we can easily remember, and easily use to turn our hearts to God as his children.

PRAYER: Lord Jesus Christ, Son of God, have mercy on us sinners.

## Friday Week 24

**2607-2614**

Jesus teaches us to pray

Parables on prayer

**2761**

The Lord's Prayer, foundation of other petitions

**2788-2789**

The Lord's Prayer: we address the Father of Jesus Christ in the oneness of the Trinity

Jesus is our model and our way of prayer. When we look to him we learn how to pray. It is through him that we are able to stand in God's presence and communicate with him as our Father.

PRAYER: Lord, we count on your steadfast love. Teach us to pray as you taught the saints before us, that you may be known in our time by all men and women.

---

## Saturday Week 24

---

2773-2776
The Lord's Prayer, the Our Father
Summary of the whole gospel

2797-2802
We are sons and daughters of God, our Father
The Lord's Prayer brings us into communion with the Father

Jesus revealed God as his Father and our Father. We could not confidently approach God this way without the words of Jesus. But since Jesus showed us the way, we have the assurance that God's heart is open to us, ready to receive us when we turn to him.

PRAYER: O God, as Jesus turned to you because you are his Father, so do I. You have wondrously shown me your everlasting love.

**238-242**
No other fatherhood is like God's
God is Father of the whole creation

**2779-2780**
Prayer to the Father
Our relationship to God as our Father through Jesus Christ, who revealed him to us

**2765**
The unique prayer given by the Lord Jesus

As God the Father is Father even within the Trinity, so he is Father of all creation. The unique relationship of God the Father and God the Son shows us much about ourselves, both our origin and our destiny.

PRAYER: God, all creation gives glory to you as its Creator and Father. To be your sons and daughters is our greatest honor.

## Monday Week 25

**475-478**
Holy images of Christ
In venerating icons we venerate the persons they depict
The Sacred Heart of Jesus

**1159-1162**
Christian iconography expresses the gospel message in images

Icons of the Mother of God and of the saints also signify Christ, who is glorified in them

In so many ways God has already allowed us to see him reflected on this earth. Yet some Christians have attacked the practice of making holy images that remind us of the presence of God, calling it idolatry. However, the Church has never treated the icon as if it were God. It is only a holy image of him whose glory fills the whole earth.

PRAYER: Father, you allowed the apostles to see your glory revealed in Christ. Open the eyes of our hearts to also recognize your presence in our lives.

---

## Tuesday Week 25

---

**1079-1083**
From the beginning, and throughout time, God's work is a blessing despite the sin of mankind

**2626-2628**
Blessing: basic movement of Christian prayer
Adoration: acknowledging we are creatures of God and exalting his greatness

Everything good comes from God as his free gift to each man and woman. His blessings are so abundant that we can scarcely recount them all. God's will is thus steadfastly oriented toward our good. By his grace we bless him in return.

PRAYER: Praise you, O Lord God. Great are your works of love. I give you thanks with all my heart.

**1430-1433**

Conversion: turning away from sin and changing one's life

Conversion comes from grace, not from the human heart by
itself

**2548-2550**

Freedom from immoderate attachment to worldly goods

Christ's faithful mortify their cravings and prevail over seductions of pleasure and power

In the Old Testament God promises through the prophet Jeremiah that he will give his people new hearts. Indeed, an interior change is exactly what we need so that our hearts will turn away from their earthly attachments and back to God.

PRAYER: Have mercy on me, O God. I need your grace to turn from sin and to return fully to you.

**2104-2109**

All are bound to seek and embrace the truth

Christians are to treat with love, prudence, and patience those in error concerning the faith

No one is to be forced to act against his convictions in religious matters

**2791-2793**

In spite of Christian divisions, the "Our Father" remains the prayer of all

To pray the Our Father is to be open to overcoming all
human divisions

The principle of religious liberty is based on the nature of
the person, created to freely give assent to truth from the
heart. When Christians turn to God as "Our Father," they
find the way to true freedom and to respect for all God's
children.

PRAYER: Father, we long to live with you as one in heaven.
Overlook all our sins of division, and show us your favor.

---

## Friday Week 25

210-213
God, the fullness of being and of every perfection
Creatures receive their being from He Who Is

2803-2806
The seven petitions of the Lord's Prayer: three directed
toward God the Father, four concerning ourselves

The profound goodness of God is beyond describing. He
is the source of all. He has his being in and of himself. It is
not received from any other. We and all creatures receive our
being from him and live in dependence on him.

PRAYER: Father, we come forth from your hand and return
to you. You have done great things for us; we rejoice in you.

2857-2865
The parts of the Our Father
Three petitions focused on the glory of the Father
Four petitions for our own needs

When Jesus taught us to pray, he placed the glory of God in first place. All of life is oriented to this, that God be glorified and honored. All that we receive, all that we do, is for the purpose of bringing praise and adoration to God our Father.

PRAYER: Our Father, who art in heaven, hallowed be thy name. Thy kingdom come, thy will be done on earth, as it is in heaven. Give us this day our daily bread, and forgive us our trespasses as we forgive those who trespass against us. Lead us not into temptation, but deliver us from evil.

**727-730**

Christ's work: joint mission of the Son and of the Holy Spirit

Jesus reveals the Holy Spirit fully after his death and resurrection

The Holy Spirit will lead us into all truth and will glorify Christ

**2615**

The Father gives us another Counselor, the Spirit of truth

Now that Christ has died and risen, the Church will always be accompanied by the Holy Spirit. How could we fulfill Christ's mission without the wisdom and power of his Spirit? With so many gifts of the Spirit in the lives of each member, the Church carries on Christ's work so that all nations will come to know him.

PRAYER: Lord, how wonderful it is to be part of your Church, that great throng who are on their way to you. Guard us always in your Spirit of love and peace.

**737-741**

The mission of Christ and the Holy Spirit is completed in the Church

Through the work of the Holy Spirit, the Church offers believers the "mighty works of God" in the sacraments

The Holy Spirit is the master of prayer

767-768

The Church is missionary by her very nature

Since his ascension into heaven, Christ has not left us alone. He promised to be with us until the end of time. Through the presence of his Holy Spirit, he continues to accompany humankind so that the visible Church, with all its faults, is really a sacrament of his presence.

PRAYER: Father, the Word you spoke through Christ your Son is with us still. By the grace of your Holy Spirit, we set our hopes on him.

---

## Tuesday Week 26

---

783-786

Sharing Christ's priestly office: consecrated to God

Sharing Christ's prophetic mission: Christ's witnesses in the world

Sharing Christ's royal office: to reign by serving

799-801

Charisms are graces of the Holy Spirit that benefit the Church

Charity is the true measure of all charisms

The wondrous works of God in our world through the Holy Spirit were not only intended for long ago or far away. Each Christian is welcomed fully into the body of Christ with a share in his priestly, prophetic, and kingly offices. A sharing in Christ's roles means the Holy Spirit is present in each Christian's life, and each may find a life of holiness and loving service within God's plan.

PRAYER: Your Word, O Lord, creates the world anew. I give you thanks for your presence in my life and in the life of the entire Church.

---

## Wednesday Week 26

1091-1098
The Holy Spirit:
  Teaches faith
  Shapes the liturgy and sacraments
  Prepares us to encounter Christ
  Unites us to the life and mission of Christ
In the liturgy we transcend all human differences
Preparing ourselves to participate in the liturgy

The harmony between the Old Covenant and the New Covenant is a work of the Holy Spirit. Christ was already present in mystery then, and he remains present in mystery now—until that time when we gather with him in heaven.

PRAYER: Thank you, Father, for bringing me from the kingdom of darkness into the kingdom of your marvelous light in Christ.

---

## Thursday Week 26

1099-1103
Anamnesis: the Holy Spirit recalls the mystery of Christ in the liturgy
The Word of God: the Holy Spirit proclaiming the meaning of the events of salvation through Scripture
The Word of God nourishes faith in our hearts

1362-1366

Liturgy: Christ's sacrifice on the cross made present and real for us now

The song asks, "Were you there when they crucified my Lord?" In one sense, all mankind was indeed present that day as Christ sacrificed his life for every person who would ever live on this earth. But we are again present at the cross when we participate in the Eucharist, which makes Christ's sacrifice present in the Church until he returns in glory.

PRAYER: Lord Jesus Christ, I turn to you in the Eucharist. I see you and hear you in this sacrament.

## Friday Week 26

1104-1109

Power of the Holy Spirit in the liturgy
The liturgy makes the events of salvation present now

1367-1368

The sacrifice of Christ and the sacrifice of the Eucharist are one
The Eucharist is also the sacrifice of the Church

The one Spirit in all members of the Church is the Holy Spirit. Though we all remain individuals and free persons, each receives the Holy Spirit, who is the one Spirit of God. Thus, especially in the liturgy, we are unified in our worship of the Father through Christ.

PRAYER: Come, Holy Spirit, fill the hearts of your faithful. Enkindle in us the fire of your love.

1110-1112
The Trinity in the liturgy:
  God the Father is adored
  Christ's saving action
  The Holy Spirit's power

1131-1134
Sacraments: efficacious signs of grace

1677-1679
Sacramentals; blessings; popular piety

Christ, the Son of God, came to restore us to a relationship with the Father. As the Son he is fully God from all eternity, but he is begotten by the Father. Thus Christ finds his source in his Father and wants us to turn to the Father as our source also.

PRAYER: Come, Holy Spirit, enlighten my mind to know God, strengthen my will to obey him, and fill my heart to love him.

1348-1355

The celebration of the Eucharist, in the presence of Christ the High Priest

The Liturgy of the Word and the homily

The Eucharistic prayer: prayer of thanksgiving and consecration

Communion: bread of heaven and cup of salvation; Body and Blood of Christ

For those who have faith to see it, the Church's liturgy is a foretaste of heaven. In the rush of life it is easy to forget these great realities we encounter in the Mass. Taking time to prepare ourselves for the liturgy beforehand will help us celebrate it more fully.

PRAYER: Lord, you feed us with your own Body and Blood that we might be nourished with your life. May our worship always be pleasing to you.

## Monday Week 27

1066-1072

Christ: Redeeming mankind and giving perfect glory to God

Liturgy: celebration of the mystery of our salvation

Celebration of worship; proclamation of the Gospel; works of charity

Church: visible sign of communion between God and man in Christ

The liturgy of the Church is more than a mere formality, more than a simple social gathering. It is not just a time when we use our minds to consider the Word of God. In the liturgy, eternal realities of God's kingdom are made present in our midst, and we participate in them with Christ.

PRAYER: Father, through your Son Jesus Christ and in the Holy Spirit we join all the saints and angels to worship you.

---

## Tuesday Week 27

1204-1206
Celebration of the liturgy to fit different cultures
Unchangeable parts of the liturgy and changeable parts
Liturgical diversity can be a source of enrichment or a source of tensions

1234-1245
The meaning and grace of the sacrament of baptism

Because Christ teaches us so, we believe that baptism brings the new Christian from the dominion of sin into the kingdom of God. The baptized person still looks the same outwardly, but by faith we know that a new life in Christ has begun.

PRAYER: Lord, we are not saved by great human strength or virtue, but by your action. We trust in you, O Lord, to hold us fast as members of your body sharing the life of your Holy Spirit.

## Wednesday Week 27

972

Mary: Icon of the Church, showing what we will be at the end of our journey in Christ

1061-1065

Amen: the way the Church ends her prayers

To believe is to say "Amen" to God and to his words, promises, and commandments

All the promises of God find their yes in Christ

The fullest Amen, the fullest yes, was given to God by Mary. As a result she already shares the glory of God in heaven, demonstrating the ultimate destiny of all who say "Amen" to God through Christ.

PRAYER: Father, you saved us from our sins for your name's sake. In gratitude, we say "Amen" to you with Christ your Son.

## Thursday Week 27

1674-1676

Popular piety and devotions: veneration of relics, visits to sanctuaries, pilgrimages, rosaries, medals, stations of the cross, religious dances

Popular piety should harmonize with the liturgy

2697-2699

Forms of prayer: morning and evening prayer, grace before and after meals, Liturgy of the Hours

Composure of the heart for prayer

So much pulls our heart away from God. A life of prayer turns us back to God, from whom we come and to whom we will return. To think of mankind without prayer would be to misunderstand who we are and what is good for us.

PRAYER: It is good to give thanks to the Lord, to sing praise to your name, O Most High.

---

## Friday Week 27

2685-2690
Christian family: first place of education in prayer; domestic Church
Religious consecrate their lives to prayer
Prayer groups as schools of prayer
Spiritual directors help others grow in prayer

2767-2772
The use of the Lord's Prayer in the Church—in baptism, confirmation, and the Eucharist

In many ways the Church grows in a life of prayer. Without specific use of the means of prayer and without the service of those who build up prayer, the Church's spiritual life would decrease.

PRAYER: Lord, teach us to pray. May your entire Church come alive in worship and prayer, with holiness of heart and holiness of life.

2692-2696
Intercession of the saints
Schools of Christian spirituality
Education for prayer in the family
Places for prayer

2720-2724
Regular prayer
Vocal, meditative, and contemplative prayer

The Church's rich heritage of prayer and approaches to spirituality is still growing. In prayer, Christians relate to God in a personal encounter that touches the depths of their hearts. Every person, every culture, can turn to the God who waits like a loving Father for his children to come to him.

PRAYER: Lord, we raise our hearts to you. Fill us with the knowledge of your presence and your kindness.

## Sunday Week 28

2705-2708
Methods of prayer, and the one way of Christ Jesus
Meditating on the mysteries of Christ

2738-2741
Trust in God, based on his Son's Passion and resurrection
The relationship of the prayer of Jesus to our prayer
Jesus' prayers on our behalf

God provides us with rich sources of prayer in the spiritualities of Christians who have gone before us, in the events of history, and in many other ways. Furthermore, he gives us the presence of his Son by our side. Jesus is our companion on our journey to the Father.

PRAYER: Lord God, we praise the greatness of your name. Hear our prayers and draw us into the life of your Son. You will be with us if we follow him.

## Monday Week 28

2700-2704
Jesus' prayers
Praying with our whole being, internal and external
Group prayer

1156-1158
The beauty of prayer in song
Song in the liturgy: unanimous participation of the assembly

God gives many gifts to his Church, and among the most precious is the gift of sacred music. Recall some of the beautiful songs of worship you have heard. Even in heaven, we are told, the saints and angels praise God with music and song.

PRAYER: Lord, teach us to pray. Move our hearts to perceive how great you are and to respond with praise worthy of your divinity.

---

## Tuesday Week 28

**538-540**
Jesus in the desert, tempted by Satan, remained faithful
Lent unites us to Christ's forty days in the desert

**1434-1439**
The many forms of penance in the Christian life
Fasting, prayer, almsgiving
Seasons and days of penance

The penance of Jesus in the desert gives us an example for penance in our own lives. The Church encourages us to imitate our Lord by acts of penance during special times and seasons—especially Lent. Christ himself said no one can be saved unless he or she does penance.

PRAYER: Change my heart, O God. I offer you my sacrifices as a sign of my humble prayer. Change my heart, O God.

470

Christ's human soul—intellect and will

The Son of God communicates his Trinitarian existence to his humanity

2600-2604

The meaning of prayer in Christ's ministry

Jesus prays before decisive moments: his Baptism, his Transfiguration, his Passion, the choice of the twelve apostles, Peter's confession of him

We learn to pray from Jesus

It would seem that if there was someone who did not need to pray, it would be Jesus Christ, who was himself God. Yet he did pray, frequently and fervently. How, then, can we overlook the need for prayer in our own lives?

PRAYER: Lord, teach us to pray; teach us to imitate you. Your entire life expressed the divine life within you.

471-474

Christ's divinity did not replace his rational, human soul

Christ had true human knowledge, which increased through experience

Christ's human nature knew and manifested everything that pertains to God

2605-2606

All human reality and prayer is summed up in Christ's last
   words from the cross

If we overemphasize Christ's divinity, then we put him on
a level that is not really human. In doing this we lower the
demands on our own lives to imitate him because there
could be no hope of imitating someone who was not really
and fully human. Thus it is important that we correctly
understand and believe what the Church teaches about
Christ as fully God and fully man.

PRAYER: Jesus Christ, you have ascended to the Father's
right hand in heaven, taking our humanity to the most
exalted state possible. Pour out on us your Holy Spirit, your
divine life and power.

---

## Friday Week 28

---

2616
Jesus hears our prayers; he understands our needs
The Jesus Prayer

2729-2731
Facing difficulties in prayer
Humble vigilance of heart in prayer
Overcoming distractions and dryness
Vigilance for the time of Jesus' coming

We must fight a spiritual battle to continue to grow in
prayer, but Christ our Lord is faithful. He loves us more than
we love ourselves, and abundantly rewards our humble
efforts to follow him.

PRAYER: Lord, we have strayed from you in many ways, yet you bring us back for your own name's sake. Support and help us in seeking you.

---

## Saturday Week 28

---

2620-2622
Christ's prayer as a model for our own
Prayer based on purity of heart, faith, boldness
Mary's prayer: the Fiat and the Magnificat

2752-2758
The battle of prayer
Distractions and dryness
Pray constantly

God wants everyone to turn to him in prayer. We do not need to think of ourselves as saints, or even as especially holy, in order to turn to him and simply tell him what we care about and what we need. There is much to learn about prayer, but we can begin at any moment.

PRAYER: Father, I lift my heart to you. I find comfort in turning to you.... (Tell God about your greatest needs.)

1140-1144

The whole body of Christ celebrates the liturgy as one

The rites of the liturgy should be celebrated with the faithful present and actively participating, not quasi-privately

All are to participate actively and consciously in the liturgy

The ordained lead the liturgy, acting in the person of Christ the Head as icons of Christ the priest

The liturgy is the high point of the life of the Church. When the body of Christ gathers, all the different ways in which each person participates add up to one reality that takes place for the common good of all. All enter into the one offering of Christ to the Father in the Holy Spirit.

PRAYER: Lord, help us to participate fully in the common worship of your Church. Bless the Church with a fullness of gifts for worship.

## Monday Week 29

1145-1152

The signs and symbols of the liturgy are based on creation and culture

Signs of the human world

Man can read traces of the Creator in the visible creation

The cosmic and symbolic meaning of religious rites

Signs of God's covenant with mankind

Christ's use of physical signs

If you encountered a new civilization, among other things you would be intrigued by their religious rituals. What did they wear? How did they use physical things like candles, water, fire, music, and the rest? How did they interact with each other? And most of all, how did they act toward God?

PRAYER: Praise God with the sound of trumpets; praise him with lute and harp. Let all that has breath praise the Lord!

---

## Tuesday Week 29

1163-1165

Liturgical seasons: recalling the mysteries and riches of Christ throughout the year

Easter and Sunday (the Lord's Day): celebrations of Christ's resurrection

Yearly celebration of Easter, most solemn Church feast

"Today!"—the time of Jesus' passover underlying all history

The Church unfolds the full mystery of Christ throughout the year: from the commemoration of his first coming at Christmas to his resurrection from the dead at Easter. In this liturgical cycle, the person of Christ is revealed to us in all the aspects of his life and truth.

PRAYER: Lord, I stand in awe of your great riches. I trust in you and I want to live for you now and forever.

1168-1171

The Easter Triduum: source of light for the liturgical year

The year is transfigured by the liturgy: the kingdom of God entering into our time

Easter: feast of feasts, the Great Sunday

In the liturgical year the various aspects of the Paschal mystery unfold

512-515

All Jesus did and taught is to be seen in the light of the mysteries of Christmas and Easter

Christ's whole life is mystery; his humanity manifests divinity

Jesus and his life on earth are summed up for us in the liturgy of the Church. By the light he sheds we come to know more and more about ourselves and about the world as he sees it.

PRAYER: O God, you awaken my soul by all the treasures of your Son Jesus. I will not be silent, but praise you forever.

## Thursday Week 29

1172-1173

The annual cycle of the liturgy marks the feasts of Mary and of the rest of the saints

Saints: examples that draw men and women to the Father through Christ

2471-2474

Christ proclaims that he has come to bear witness to the truth

Christians are to be witnesses of the gospel

Martyrdom: supreme witness to Christ, to the point of death

So many people are inspired by the stories of the saints, these men and women whose lives and deeds were a testimony to something greater, something holy. Through their living witness our hearts are touched and opened to God.

PRAYER: Great is the Lord in the lives of his disciples. Father, you give joy to the earth through your holy ones.

---

## Friday Week 29

---

1174-1178

The Liturgy of the Hours, "the divine office":

Made up of hymns, litanies, readings from the Word of God, readings from the Church fathers, psalms

Making the course of each day holy

Intended for the whole People of God

Leads to adoration of the Blessed Sacrament

The rosary grew out of a desire on the part of lay people to share in the prayer of the monasteries. Copies of the Psalms were rare, and thus people prayed 150 Hail Marys—one for each psalm. The same urge to sanctify the course of each day motivated all of Christ's followers, just as it motivated the monks whose entire lives were consecrated by vows. Now that the Psalms are readily available, it is easier to extend the use of the Liturgy of the Hours to more members of the Church.

PRAYER: O God, I join my prayers of praise to those of the entire Church in union with Christ our Lord; together with one voice we praise you.

---

## Saturday Week 29

1187-1199
Liturgy: work of the whole body of Christ
Baptismal priesthood and ordained priesthood
Signs and symbols in the liturgy
Song, music, sacred images
Sunday, the "Lord's Day"
Liturgical year and feasts of the saints
Liturgy of the Hours
Church buildings

The elements of church life associated with the worship of God form a rich tapestry to which all the ages of the Church have contributed. We benefit from the art and music, and the holiness, of the Christians who have gone before us—and we now enter into that same great praise of the Father, which will go on until the end of time.

PRAYER: Lord, I rejoice that the Church calls me to join in praising you. I bring my entire life to you in the liturgy—all that I have and all that I am.

1440, 1442-1449
Sacrament of Penance and Reconciliation
The apostles' power of absolution
Jesus receives sinners at his table
Reconciliation with God and with the Church are inseparable
The sacrament: contrition, confession, and satisfaction

The mercy of God calls us to come to Jesus in the first place, but also to be restored to him if we have turned away. Christ opens his heart to receive back our wayward hearts. Turn to him now and receive his forgiveness.

PRAYER: Lord, no matter how great my sins, you cleanse me of them all. Though I have darkened my heart, your light chases every shadow away. May your mercy come to me always.

1450-1454
Contrition: sorrow for sin and resolution not to sin again
Perfect contrition and imperfect contrition
Examination of conscience

1480-1484
Words of absolution
Communal celebration of the sacrament
Individual confession and absolution

When the priest in the sacrament of Penance absolves us of our sins, he does so in the person of Christ himself. Christ mysteriously present is the active agent, removing our sins and reconciling us to the Father. We can always approach the priest confident of Christ's presence and mercy.

PRAYER: Lord, forgive my many sins. Thank you for this sacrament by which I can be renewed in my relationship with you and with your Father.

## Tuesday Week 30

1461-1467

Bishops and priests have the power to forgive sins in the sacrament of Penance

Automatic excommunication for particularly grave sins

The Good Shepherd seeks the lost sheep

The "sacramental seal"—no priest may reveal what he has heard in confession

1567-1568

Priests share the ministry of their bishop

Brotherhood of all priests with each other

Unity and love among priests make a powerful impact on the faithful. Their relationship with one another inspires people to have confidence in God and in the Church, and it attracts others to serve alongside them.

PRAYER: Lord, thank you for our priests. Preserve them in their faithfulness to you and allow them to grow in holiness.

1468-1470
Effects of the sacrament of Penance:
   Restoration to God's grace
   Restoration to a good relationship with the Church

1520-1523
Effects of the sacrament of the Anointing of the Sick:
   Gift of the Holy Spirit to handle serious illness or frailty
   Union with the Passion of Christ
Preparation for the final journey of death

The Church, through the will of Christ, offers us help with illness of body and soul. When our health is seriously threatened, the mercy of God can come very close to us through the Anointing of the Sick. When we need to be reconciled to God because of serious sin, he stands ready to receive us in the sacrament of Penance.

PRAYER: Father, when my soul is bowed down with suffering and sin, you touch me and renew my spirit. Let your light ever shine into this world's darkness.

1471-1473
Indulgence: under certain conditions set by the Church, a
   remission of the temporal punishment due to sin
The consequences of sin

Purification in purgatory frees us from the temporal punishment of sin

2634-2636
Intercession: asking on behalf of another
Sharing Christ's role as an intercessor

As our hearts become more like Christ's, we have a greater care for the needs of others. Having experienced God's mercy ourselves, we grow in mercy for others. Interceding for others and gaining indulgences for those in purgatory are two ways we can express this mercy.

PRAYER: Lord, you never forget our afflictions. Give us your own heart to always care for others in their afflictions.

---

## Friday Week 30

---

1474-1479
The supernatural unity of the Mystical Body of Christ
The exchange of spiritual goods between the Church in heaven, in purgatory, and on earth
The Church's spiritual treasury is of infinite value
Indulgences and the Church's power of binding and loosing

2346-2347
Chastity leads those who practice it to become witnesses to God's faithfulness

The followers of Christ have a real relationship with all others who follow Christ, and in a different way with all mankind. In Christ, they build each other up spiritually as well as materially.

PRAYER: Lord, have mercy on those who are in purgatory. Arouse our hearts to love them by seeking indulgences on their behalf.

---

## Saturday Week 30

1485-1498
The sacrament of Penance
Sorrow for sins and confession to a priest
Necessity of confessing mortal sins
Firm purpose of sinning no more
Acts of penance

God is rich in mercy and wants us to be saved from our sins. Even when we turn from him in sin, he offers us a way back through the sacrament of Penance. It is by the power of his grace that we return to communion with him.

PRAYER: Father, I reject sin. I determine to turn from all the enticements of Satan. In your mercy, restore what I have lost through disobeying you.

1846-1848
Jesus, Savior for sinners
Admitting our faults
God casts light, exposing the darkness of sin

2842-2845
To forgive others as God forgives us
Forgiveness of enemies
No limit to divine forgiveness

Jesus teaches that we cannot expect mercy if we are unmerciful to others. We become people of mercy by the transformation of our hearts in Christ and in his Holy Spirit. A genuine and consistent mercy is one of the greatest reflections of God in the world.

PRAYER: O Lord, you are so merciful. We need you and your unfailing love. Hold us fast in your great kindness.

386-387
Presence of sin in human history

2846-2849
Trials are necessary for the growth of the inner man
Discernment between trials, temptations, and consent to temptation
God is faithful and will not let you be tempted beyond your strength

A hallmark of our times is a general loss of the sense of sin. One of God's purposes in intervening in our history is precisely to open our eyes to our own state of sin—so that we can say, like the man in the back of the synagogue, "Lord, have mercy on me a sinner."

PRAYER: Lord, I thank you with all my heart for opening my eyes to my own sin and to your love. I count on your mercy.

## Tuesday Week 31

1762-1766
Passions incline us to act or not act in regard to good and evil
The passions include love, hatred, aversion, fear, sadness, anger

2514-2516
Ninth commandment
Concupiscence: rebellion of the "flesh" against the "spirit," a result of the sin of our first parents

One of the reasons for the daily battles of human life is that human beings are not completely sound within themselves. Even if all external circumstances were in order, we would still face struggles of sin because of the flaws in our own being. This ongoing struggle calls for a vigilant turning to Christ, source of grace for a new way of life.

PRAYER: Lord, have mercy on me a sinner. I trust in you and I rejoice that you have embraced me in your righteousness.

**1767-1770**
Perfection: to govern our passions by reason
The Holy Spirit mobilizes the entire person, including the passions

**2517-2519**
Both good and evil come out of the heart
The pure in heart have attuned their intellects and wills to God's holiness

Bringing our strongest passions into conformity with what is good is the work of a lifetime. It is not just a distasteful labor, however, because the power of habit makes our efforts progressively more fruitful. Each good action makes us richer in dispositions of truth and charity.

PRAYER: Lord, I study your ways because they are the ways of life. Enkindle in me a fire of love for you and your truth.

**2520-2524**
The baptized continue to struggle against their own divided desires
Aids to purity: chastity, purity of intention and of vision, prayer

**2348-2350**
All the baptized are called to chastity in different forms: in marriage, in single life, in consecrated life

Chastity during engagement

In our permissive society the implication is often given that the chaste are overly concerned with purity. But Christ's call is total, and those who follow it are the ones who are ready to serve their Master with undivided hearts.

PRAYER: Christ, I choose the better part, I choose you. Hold me fast as your own disciple and guide me to a life pleasing to you.

## Friday Week 31

1606-1608
The effects of sin within marriages

2351-2356
Sexual pleasure is disordered when it is isolated from its procreative and unitive purposes
Masturbation is a gravely disordered action
Fornication is contrary to the dignity of persons
Pornography does grave injury to its participants and to society
Prostitution reduces a person to an instrument of sexual pleasure
Rape is intrinsically evil

The greater and more noble something is, the more ignoble is its corruption. Thus sexuality corrupted leads to the ugly realities of rape, prostitution, pornography, and so on. When sexuality is properly used, however, it leads to the great reality of the union of a man and a woman in a family bearing new human life.

PRAYER: O God, your goodness shines forth through the love of man and woman. May all marriages and all families know the presence of your grace and your love.

## Saturday Week 31

2528-2533
Ninth commandment
Lust and concupiscence
Temperance
Purity of heart and modesty

Sin starts in the heart when we covet what is not rightfully ours. Second Samuel 11 tells the story of David looking on Bathsheba from his window and coveting her. This sin led to adultery and even to murder, illustrating why God commands us not to let sin begin in our hearts.

PRAYER: Lord, cleanse me of my sin; wash me and I shall again be pleasing to you. Fill my heart with holy desires to serve you.

2360-2363

Sexuality was created for the conjugal love of man and woman

Sexuality is not simply biological for human beings but concerns the innermost person

Union of spouses and the transmission of life cannot be separated

1649-1651

Though the Church may permit husband and wife to physically separate, they remain indissolubly husband and wife

If there is separation, reconciliation is the best goal to seek

A divorced and remarried person may not receive Communion or exercise ecclesial responsibilities, but he or she can and should participate in the Church in other ways

Today's society tends to separate the pleasures of sexual relationships from the reality of bringing new children into the world. This has been referred to as the "contraceptive mentality." Up until early in the twentieth century, all Christian churches held that this was wrong. Even Freud asserted that sexual perversion consisted in separating sexual acts from procreation. The current mentality of society on these matters cannot be upheld by natural reasoning or by the teaching of the Church.

PRAYER: Lord, may our marriages reflect your love and holiness. Your ways are the ways of truth and goodness. We praise and thank you for them.

## Monday Week 32

1621-1624
The appropriateness of celebrating marriage during Mass
The spouses confer the sacrament on each other in the Latin Church
In Eastern Churches the priest or bishop is the minister of this sacrament

2201-2203
The nature of the family
Public authority has an obligation to recognize the family

Marriage and the family are not just a good idea discovered by men and women. They come from the hand of God. No one, neither private individual nor head of government, may disregard these realities or try to undo them. The good of individuals and the common good of societies depend on respect for God's institution.

PRAYER: O God, how great is your wisdom. Open our hearts and our minds to know your ways for our happiness.

## Tuesday Week 32

711-716
Isaiah foretells the Messiah's characteristics, especially in the "Servant songs"
Christ accepts Isaiah's prophecy: "The Spirit of the Lord is upon me"

2232-2233

The family must recognize and accept each child's unique God-given vocation

The first vocation of the Christian is to follow Jesus

Parents should welcome the Lord's call of their children to consecrated life or priesthood

God has a specific vocation in mind for each of us. Just as the vocation of Jesus was prepared ahead of time, so is ours. When we accept our vocation as he accepted his, we find that his plans for us are always greater than our own.

PRAYER: Lord, hear my voice. You know me, you see me. Open my heart and mind to know you, to see you, and to follow you.

---

## Wednesday Week 32

---

2197-2200

After God we are to honor our parents

The reward for obedience of the fourth commandment is temporal peace and prosperity

2214-2217

Divine fatherhood is the source of human fatherhood

Respect for parents derives from gratitude for all they have given us

God's plan is not to leave us orphans. He brings us into the world in the context of a relationship with those who are able to care for us and introduce us to life and to the truth about life. Thus we are asked to honor them, since he has set them over us for our good.

PRAYER: O Lord, you are a great and wonderful Father. How good you are to us, your children. Bless our families that they might live in truth and love.

## Thursday Week 32

**2204-2206**

Domestic church: ecclesial communion at home in the family

Christian family: an image of the communion of Father, Son, and Holy Spirit

The family reflects creation in the birth of new children; it reflects redemption in prayer and Scripture reading

**527-530**

Jesus' circumcision as prefiguration of baptism

Mysteries within Jesus' earthly family life: the Epiphany, the presentation in the temple, the flight into Egypt

The family was present at the time of creation in Adam and Eve, and at the time of redemption in the family of Nazareth. In eternity the family will remain—in the relationship of Christ with his bride the Church, and in the relationship of all to God the Father.

PRAYER: Lord Jesus, be present in our families today as you were present with Joseph and Mary at Nazareth. You give meaning to all the details of daily life.

2218-2220

Responsibilities of grown children toward their parents

Gratitude to those from whom we have received the gift of faith and baptism

2225-2231

Responsibility of parents to evangelize their children and bring them into the Church

Children can contribute to their parents' growth in holiness

Parents' rights to choose a school for their children

When children become adults they have the right to choose their own profession and state of life

Our society tends to think that the most important goods are those an individual may attain on his own. As a result, people often overlook the great treasures that can be achieved only in and through a rich family and social life.

PRAYER: Father, you did not create us to achieve holiness on our own but by communion of life with others. Give us a share of the life you share as Father, Son, and Holy Spirit.

2247-2257

Fourth commandment: Honor your father and mother

Marriage covenant for the good of the spouses and the procreation and education of children

Children's duties to parents

Parents' duties in regard to their children

Duties of public authorities

Christian tradition has always understood the fourth commandment to address every relationship of human authority. Christ himself is the model of authority, in that he came not to be served but to serve. Thus, for example, the authority of parents over their children is for the good of the children, that they might be formed in a life that is worthy of sons and daughters of God.

PRAYER: Father, when we care for others, allow us to do it as you would. Help us to overcome our failings and faithfully serve those you put in our charge.

1601-1605

The sacrament of matrimony

God is the author of marriage; it is not a purely human institution

Each culture has a sense of the greatness of marriage

The love between man and woman is an image of God's love

As the *Catechism* points out, the beginning of Scripture tells the story of man and woman made for each other in the vocation of marriage, and the end of Scripture shows our destiny in the wedding feast of the Lamb. Earthly marriages come to an end with the death of one spouse, but we are destined to participate in the wedding of Christ and his Church, which lasts for all eternity.

PRAYER: Lord Jesus, you have shown yourself faithful to us, like the perfect bridegroom. Happy are we whom you have chosen.

372

Man and woman were made to be a communion of persons, equal and complementary

Man and woman transmit life in marriage—unique cooperation in God's creative work

1643-1648

Indissolubility, faithfulness, openness to fertility

Equal personal dignity of husband and wife
Polygamy is contrary to conjugal love

God made mankind male and female for mutual love and procreation. He gave us the great dignity of participating with him in the creation and formation of new human lives. We need his wisdom and grace to fulfill our roles in this wonderful plan.

PRAYER: God, your plan for human life shows forth your goodness and love. We receive your love gladly. May we reflect it to others.

---

## Tuesday Week 33

---

1625-1632
The free consent of the spouses makes the marriage
The consent of the two spouses is fulfilled in their becoming one flesh
The importance of good preparation for marriage, especially through the example and teaching of parents

2364-2365
Marriage: intimate partnership of life and love established by the Creator

Marriage is said to be a partnership of life and love because it is in the context of the love of husband and wife that God intends new human life to enter the world. Just as every living thing will thrive in the right setting, so will the new human person thrive in the setting of love.

PRAYER: Father, guard and guide every marriage. May our families be environments of true love in Christ.

## Wednesday Week 33

**1652-1654**

Marriage and married love are ordered to the procreation and education of children

Spouses without children can be fruitful in charity, hospitality, and sacrifice

**2373-2379**

Large families are a blessing and a sign of generosity

The suffering of sterility

Guidelines for fertility research

Artificial insemination is morally unacceptable

A child is a gift, not a right

Any marriage closed to new life, closed to the possibility of children, is not what a marriage is supposed to be. At the same time, seeking to bear a child outside the means designed by God is a violation of the rights of children.

PRAYER: Lord, it is a great wonder that you associate us with your own work in the creation of new life. May the next generation come to know and love you.

## Thursday Week 33

**1609-1614**

Since the Fall, marriage has helped men and women to overcome self-absorption and egoism

Jesus' first miraculous sign was in the context of a wedding celebration

Jesus taught the original meaning of the union of men and
women

2380-2381
Adultery, forbidden by the sixth commandment, is an injustice

God's will is that the marriage covenant between a man
and a woman last as long as both are alive. This is an obvious
need for the sake of children, but it also reflects something
we know only by faith: the fidelity of Christ and the Church
to each other, which will continue throughout eternity.

PRAYER: Lord, may your Spirit reign in our marriages and
in our families. Teach us your faithfulness.

---

## Friday Week 33

---

1633-1642
The great difficulties of mixed marriage, especially as regards
education of the children
The perpetual and exclusive bond of marriage is a sacrament
for Christians
A marriage concluded and consummated between baptized
persons cannot be dissolved
Love and family life: a foretaste of the wedding feast of the
Lamb in heaven

The marriage of two baptized Catholics shares in the
reality of the union of Christ and his Church. Christ himself is present in the home, so it is really a vital part of the
Church. Thus marriage with spouses other than Catholics

are carefully pastored by the Church.

PRAYER: Christ, strengthen the marriages of the Church. Help us to be faithful to one another and to be a sign of your love in the midst of a world that does not follow your ways.

---

## Saturday Week 33

1659-1666
Marriage, covenant and sacrament
Intimate communion of life and love
Unity, indissolubility, openness to fertility
Divorce and remarriage
The domestic church: the Christian home

Marriage was founded by God at the beginning of human creation, and it was raised by Christ to the dignity of a sacrament reflecting the union of Christ with his Church. The Christian home, built on this sacrament, occupies a privileged place in the Church and in society.

PRAYER: Lord, bless the children of all the families of the Church. May each home be a place where they are able to know you and love you.

## Sunday Week 34

369-371, 373
God created man and woman together and for each other
Man and woman have the vocation of sovereignty over the earth as God's stewards
2331-2336
Sixth commandment: You shall not commit adultery, even in your heart
Sexuality affects all aspects of the human person

God created men and women for a vocation of love, to live in communion with each other. Their differences and complementarity suit them for their vocation to cooperate with God and each other in all the duties of marriage and family.

PRAYER: O God, we have received a great inheritance from you. May we be your faithful servants in family life and in all our relationships.

## Monday Week 34

1615-1617
Christ gives the grace to live the indissolubility of marriage
Husbands are to love their wives as Christ loves the Church

2382-2386
Marriage between a baptized man and a baptized woman cannot be dissolved by any human power
Separation of a married couple is permitted in certain cases

Divorce is a grave offense against Natural Law

A spouse unjustly abandoned by his or her partner has not
broken the moral law

No matter how compatible a particular man and woman
are, still they are part of the fallen human race, and as a result
they face many incompatibilities. Like all goods in life, the
state of marriage requires the grace of Christ.

PRAYER: Lord, we have turned from you so often, like an
adulterous spouse. Yet you remain faithful to us and show us
a way to overcome our sins.

---

## Tuesday Week 34

---

2337-2345

Chastity: successful integration of sexuality, insuring the unity
of the person

Sexuality is truly human in the complete and lifelong mutual
gift of a man and a woman

Sexual self-mastery, training in human freedom: a long and
exacting work

The power of sexuality is related to the profound depths
of the person. Those who guard their sexuality in a chaste
fashion are prepared to make a fully human gift of themselves
to another person of the opposite sex in marriage, and ultimately to Christ, the Bridegroom of the soul.

PRAYER: Lord, you have called us to your glorious and
eternal wedding feast in heaven. Come, Lord Jesus.

**2357-2359**

Homosexual acts are gravely disordered and under no circumstances can they be approved

The origin of homosexual tendencies remains largely unexplained

Persons with homosexual tendencies are to be accepted with respect and compassion

**2541-2543**

Law and grace turn men's hearts from sinful desires to the desires of the Holy Spirit

The Church's teaching on homosexuality requires understanding and respect for homosexual persons and their rights while rejecting homosexual acts. Homosexual persons are called to live chastely, as are all Christians, who can turn to the Holy Spirit for the grace to follow Christ's ways.

PRAYER: Lord, you said, "Take my yoke upon you, and learn from me.... For my yoke is easy and my burden is light" (Mt 11:29-30). Surely your ways are the ways of happiness.

**2366-2372**

Married love naturally tends to be fruitful

Parental generosity and the regulation of births

The conjugal act necessarily includes both unitive and procreative dimensions

Regulation of births based on natural methods
Transmitting human life has eternal significance
The state may intervene in its demographics as long as it
    honors the moral law and the rights of spouses

One of the chief challenges of our age is the so-called sexual revolution. In the face of this challenge, it becomes more and more clear how wise is the Church's teaching about sexuality and marriage.

PRAYER: Lord, open our minds to your truth. Your ways protect us from evil. Help us follow you.

---

## Friday Week 34

---

2387-2391
Offenses against the dignity of marriage
Polygamy, contrary to equal personal dignity of man and
    woman
Incest, an especially grave offense
Sexual abuse
Trial marriage, violation of total and definitive self-giving

In God's plan, marriage partakes of the greatest human dignity. Thus, offenses against it are of the gravest sort: adultery, incest, polygamy. What may seem like a small sin at the time can have very destructive results. On the other hand, the more we follow God's ways, the more we will experience our dignity as his sons and daughters.

PRAYER: Lord, have mercy on all those who are trapped in patterns of abuse of marriage. Care for all whose lives are harmed when your ways are ignored.

**2392-2400**
Sixth commandment: You shall not commit adultery
Mankind created as man and woman, in equal dignity
Chastity and sins against chastity
Faithfulness and childbearing in marriage

Love is the vocation of every human being, a vocation lived out by most people within marriage. God's gift of sexuality is designed for the fulfillment of this vocation between husband and wife. Adultery, on the other hand, amounts to a rejection of this vocation and a violation of the mutual gift of self expressed sexually in marriage.

PRAYER: Lord Jesus, you are our great teacher of loyalty and justice. Be present in our families so that our homes and relationships may be filled with joy and love.

**1533-1535**

The sacraments of initiation lead to our common vocation as Christ's disciples

Holy Orders and Matrimony lead to different missions

**1539-1543**

Priesthood of the Old Covenant: prefiguration of New Testament ordained ministry

Prayers used in the ordination of bishops, priests, deacons

Within his people God sets apart some to serve him and his people as priests. Others he calls to serve him through marriage. By his grace in both of these calls God builds his Church in holiness and love.

PRAYER: Father, all the earth and its inhabitants are yours. Give us pure hearts to serve each other in the missions you give each of us.

**1544-1545, 1547**

The priesthood of the Old Covenant prefigured Christ's unique priestly sacrifice on the cross

Baptismal priesthood of all the faithful; ministerial or hierarchical priesthood of bishops and priests

**2623-2625**

The gift of the Holy Spirit at Pentecost forms the Church in prayer

Prayers from Scripture, especially the Psalms

The priesthood of the ordained brings the priesthood of the faithful alive by making the Eucharist and the other sacraments possible for all of us. Through the service of the priest, everyone may enter fully into each sacrament.

PRAYER: Father, I join my prayers to those of the entire Church in the Eucharist. With one voice we praise you and thank you for your great works of salvation.

## Tuesday Week 35

876-879
Ecclesial ministry: character of service and of collegiality; personal character
Christ took the form of a slave for us
Bishops exercise their office within the episcopal college and in communion with the Bishop of Rome

1536-1538
Holy Orders: the sacrament of apostolic ministry
The ordained exercise sacred power which comes from Christ through his Church

The role of the ordained—bishops, priests, and deacons—is a role of service. Christ set the pattern for leadership in his body: he laid down his life for others. In following his model of leadership, the ordained become servants of the rest of his brothers and sisters.

PRAYER: Lord, you came humbly in our midst, not dominating us, but serving us even to the point of death. Help us to follow your example.

**1548-1551**

Christ himself is present to the Church in the service of the ordained

The presence of Christ in the ordained minister does not mean that the minister is preserved from all human weaknesses and sins

An ordained minister's sins cannot impede the grace of the sacraments

**1554**

The three degrees of Holy Orders: deacon, priest, bishop

Christ sent those who have received Holy Orders to us to accomplish many things. They are his messengers though they remain our fellow human beings. They have been sent in a unique way to serve us in the place of Christ.

PRAYER: Lord Jesus Christ, bless our bishops, priests, and deacons, that they might worthily serve you. Give them the strength they need to make your name known.

**1552-1553**

Priests are not delegates of the Church community but representatives of Christ the Head

**1555-1561**

Apostolic succession

Consecration of the bishop: fullness of the sacrament of Holy
Orders
Collegial nature of the episcopal order

The group of apostles formed a unity together, not just a
set of similar individual servants of Christ. That unified group
is still with us as the college of bishops, for the apostles at
Christ's direction added others to their group through ordination. The college of bishops will remain with us, represent-
ing Christ, until Christ himself comes again.

PRAYER: Lord Jesus, we want to know you more and more.
Thank you for coming to us through your ordained ministers
that we might find you more fully.

---

## Friday Week 35

1562-1566
Priests: coworkers with the bishops, sharing in Christ's
authority
The sacrament of Holy Orders configures priests to Christ
Supreme exercise of priesthood: the Eucharistic assembly

1587
Prayer of ordination from the Byzantine Rite

1589
The urgent call to conversion for priests so that they may
worthily represent Christ

While there are many exceptions, Catholics overall have
lost a degree of respect for their priests. Emphasizing the

brotherly relationship with them has tended to obscure the uniqueness of their role. Within the Church, they represent Christ, the Head of the body, in a way the laity do not.

PRAYER: Christ, our High Priest, send laborers into your harvest. Help us all to encourage vocations for the sake of your Church.

---

## Saturday Week 35

1590-1600
The common priesthood of the faithful
The ministerial priesthood of the ordained
The sacred powers of bishops, presbyters, and deacons
Ordination only for men
Celibacy for the love of God's kingdom

King Henry VIII outlawed Catholic priests in England when he broke away from unity with the Pope. Henry understood that the Church would be most threatened if its shepherds were eliminated. However, many courageous priests braved the threat of death to continue to bring the sacraments to Christ's followers.

PRAYER: Lord, so often we take your grace for granted. Give us a renewed appreciation for every sacrament you make available to us through your ministers.

**1569-1574**
Ordination of deacons
Deacons' tasks
Restoration of the permanent diaconate since Vatican II
Ordinations of bishops, priests, and deacons should take place on Sundays, in the cathedral, with solemnity
The essential rite for all ordinations consists of the bishop's imposition of hands with the prayers of consecration

**1588**
Deacons serve in the liturgy, the gospel, and works of charity

Ordinations have always been solemn events in the life of the Church. In the case of the apostles themselves, Christ spent the night in prayer before naming those who would be the first priests and bishops of the New Covenant. Even now, a day of ordinations is a great time of celebration for an entire diocese.

PRAYER:  Lord, you have raised up salvation for us in so many ways. Let us always see your face in your holy priests and bishops.

**208-209**
The holiness of God and his name

**2809-2812**
By sin man fell short of the glory of God

Restoration of the image of God in man
God's holy people
God's people's failures
Faithfulness of Jesus Christ

Holiness comes from God alone. It is unique to the Father, Son, and Holy Spirit. God wants to share his life with us, but to share his life, we also must become holy. Thus, the holiness of God is one of the essential marks of his people the Church.

PRAYER: Holy, holy, holy Lord God Almighty. Heaven and earth are filled with your glory. Help me to change my life by your grace that I might also walk in holiness of life.

---

## Tuesday Week 36

---

203-207
God makes his name known to make himself known
Revelation of God's name to Moses at the burning bush
"I Am Who I Am"

2807-2808
Asking the Father that his name be made holy: "Hallowed be thy name"
God reveals his name as he performs his works on earth

Imagine living without knowing God or how to speak of him. Without his revelation, of himself and of his name, we would still be wandering in the dark, not knowing how to think of our Creator.

PRAYER: Father, may your name be known by all men and women. May all love you and honor your name. Now that you have revealed yourself to us, lead us on to fullness of life in you.

---

## Wednesday Week 36

---

243-248
Father and Son revealed by the Holy Spirit
Holy Spirit, Lord and giver of life
With the Father and Son, the Holy Spirit is worshipped and
glorified
The Holy Spirit proceeds from the Father and the Son

2766
The Holy Spirit guides our prayer

The Holy Spirit is the third Person of the Trinity, fully God with the Father and the Son. The Holy Spirit shares everything in the plan of the Father, and in the work of the Son. And the Holy Spirit fills the hearts of the faithful.

PRAYER: Come, Holy Spirit, fill my heart and grant that I may know the Father and the Son and be aflame with the greatness of their love.

249-256

Teaching about the Trinity was clarified in the early Church
Terminology for the Trinity: substance, person, relation
The three Persons and their relationship with each other
Complete unity of the three distinct Persons of the Trinity

The great street preacher Frank Sheed said he received the most response from his listeners when he spoke about the Trinity. Our God, in whose likeness we are made, is three Persons yet one God. Each of the three Persons is different, but all are fully God.

PRAYER: O God, Father, Son, and Holy Spirit, bring me into your shared life, your shared love. You are one God, from whom all good things come.

257-260

The divine works and Trinitarian missions
Christian life: communion with the three Persons of the
    Trinity
We become a dwelling place for the Holy Trinity

1996-1998

Grace: God's favor undeserved
Grace: participation in the life of God

The life to which God raises us is supernatural, and thus beyond our own capacities. It is a life in which we can do what is otherwise impossible for human beings.

PRAYER: O Holy Trinity, come and dwell in me. May I grow in communion with you each day of my life.

---

## Saturday Week 36

---

261-267
The Trinity
Incarnation of God's Son
Mission of the Holy Spirit
By baptism we share in the life of the Trinity

960-962
Unity of believers in the one body of Christ
Communion of saints

Even though there are three divine Persons, God is One. This unity is reflected in the oneness of all Christians in Christ. It is because we are all incorporated into him that we have communion with one another.

PRAYER: Lord Jesus, you prayed that your followers would be united so that the world would know you were sent by the Father. Guide the leaders of your Church to find ways of overcoming every separation that comes from our sin.

26
I believe/We believe
The search for the meaning of life

1701-1709
Christ reveals man to himself
The divine image in every person, dignity of the person
Original sin, overcome by Christ
In Christ: adoption as sons of God

The life of faith is a complete revolution from the life dominated by original sin. The meaning of life gains an absolute reference in Christ because through Christ we are related to God, the Lord of all.

PRAYER: Lord Jesus Christ, hold me fast. I come to you as a sinner in need of new life. In you I find redemption and the purpose of my life.

519-521
Jesus is our model
Christ enables us to live in him, and he lives in us

1691-1696
Christian, recognize your dignity and live a life worthy of the gospel of Christ
Christians: dead to sin and alive to God in Christ Jesus
The two ways: of life and of death

Through suffering and trial Christ was faithful to his Father and set an example for us. Looking beyond the sacrifices of the present, he set his eyes on heaven. We are pleasing to God when we imitate him.

PRAYER: Father, when we see Jesus we see you; and through him you are with us. He is our Way, our Truth, and our Life.

---

## Tuesday Week 37

---

516-518
Christ's entire life is a mystery of revelation, redemption, and recapitulation

1425-1426
Christians: in Christ yet still sinners
The frailty of human nature remains after baptism
Concupiscence, the inclination to sin
The ongoing struggle of conversion

Christ revealed something entirely new to the human race: God's complete forgiveness and a new humanity in Christ. In a sense this new reality is complete. But in another sense those who follow Christ must continue to achieve it daily by ongoing conversion.

PRAYER: Lord, my days come from your hand as an opportunity to come closer to you. Change my heart that I may belong completely to you.

1999-2005
Sanctifying grace
Habitual and actual grace
Preparation for grace
Graces in each sacrament
Graces of one's state in life

Man is unable to be fulfilled in this world alone. We were created with a capacity to share God's life, and we are only complete and happy if we do. Our share in his life is called grace. It is a wonderful free gift, just as our natural human life is a gift.

PRAYER: Lord, my soul rests in you. I want to share your life. Help me rise above the temptations of this world and walk more closely with you each day.

2813-2815
Baptism: sanctification and justification
Prayer in the name of Jesus

2012-2016
All Christians are called to holiness
Spiritual progress: ever more intimate union with Christ
The way of holiness: the way of the cross

The Second Vatican Council clarified that all Christians, no matter what their walk of life, are called to live in holiness.

Holiness is not only for priests and nuns but for every Christian home, for doctors, carpenters, farmers, musicians, housewives, and for all.

PRAYER: Father, I no longer belong to myself but to you. May your will be foremost in my mind and heart. Transform my life to be like yours.

---

## Friday Week 37

2006-2011
Merit
God associates mankind with his works of grace
Our adoption as God's sons is a cause of true merit
Charity of Christ: source in us of all our merits

Merit with God does not work like merit with our fellow human beings. Since God is the source of our life and of all the good we do, we have no merits before him that are attributable to our own independent action. Yet when we live God's way, even though all our goodness comes from his grace, our lives are worthy of merit in his eyes.

PRAYER: Father, I know you have done good in me through Christ and by the power of your Holy Spirit. For my part, I implore your grace that I might imitate you more fully than ever before, and seek you above everything.

2017-2029

Sharers in the life of Christ and the righteousness of God by the power of the Holy Spirit

Justification: forgiveness and renewal of the inner man, merited by Christ's Passion

Sanctifying grace; merit; Christian perfection

When we humbly turn to God, seeking forgiveness like the man in the back of the synagogue who quietly beat his breast in repentance, then Christ ushers us into the wonders of his grace. Then we have the great joy to hear him say, "Come, follow me."

PRAYER: Lord, may all see and understand that it is you who have made us new. Now that we share your life, we want to share it to the fullest, pleasing you in all things.

**683-686**

The Holy Spirit, source of our relationship with Christ in faith

The Holy Spirit, the last member of the Trinity to be revealed

**702-704**

The Father's Word and Spirit at work in the times of the Old Testament

The Word and Breath of God in creation

Wherever there is faith, wherever we encounter Christ, there the Holy Spirit of God is also present. The Holy Spirit was key to our physical creation, but he is also key to our rebirth in Christ. He is the Lord and Giver of life.

PRAYER: Lord, have mercy on me. Do not take your Holy Spirit away from me; he is my life.

## Monday Week 38

**687-688**

The Holy Spirit dwells in us and disposes us to receive Christ

The Holy Spirit is known in Scripture, tradition, the Magisterium, the sacraments, prayer, and so on.

**1285-1287**

Sacrament of confirmation, completion of baptismal grace

The fullness of the Holy Spirit was communicated to the whole messianic people

The first Pentecost

The presence of the Holy Spirit is real though entirely mysterious. As Jesus said, the action of the Spirit is like the wind: we don't know where it comes from or where it will go. In fact, the Holy Spirit often goes entirely unnoticed. But the wonderful effects of the Spirit's work are noticed—in renewed human lives, in desire to serve and worship God, in rekindled hope.

PRAYER: O Holy Spirit, fill my heart. Make me more and more like Jesus. Renew my life in God.

---

## Tuesday Week 38

---

731-736
The outpouring of the Holy Spirit on the Day of Pentecost
Forgiveness of sins and restoration of the divine likeness
The fruit of the Holy Spirit

1302-1305
Sacrament of confirmation:
>   Full outpouring of the Holy Spirit, increase of baptismal grace, more perfect bond with the Church
>   We become witnesses of Christ, with power to profess our faith
>   Indelible spiritual mark on the soul

The Holy Spirit is given to Christians now as he has been given since the Day of Pentecost. The Spirit transforms us interiorly, giving us new hearts. The Holy Spirit also gives us the power to represent Christ outwardly to others.

PRAYER: O Holy Spirit, console us when our hearts are discouraged. May your love be poured into our hearts, for we thirst for you.

---

## Wednesday Week 38

---

691-693
Christ revealed the name of the Holy Spirit
The inexpressible Third Person of the Trinity
Titles of the Holy Spirit: the Paraclete, the Consoler, the
    Spirit of Truth

1288-1289
Anointing with oil to signify the gift of the Holy Spirit
The name of the sacrament: Confirmation in the Western
    Church; Chrismation in the Eastern Church

God the Father and God the Son bear names that are reflected in visible realities in our world. Though they are not exactly like fathers and sons in our world, these words give us a strong image of the nature of these two Persons of the Trinity. We have no specific image of the Third Person, however. What we do know is that Jesus called him the Holy Spirit and that the Church has defined his full participation in the Trinity as a Person equal to the Father and Son.

PRAYER: Holy Spirit, inspire us to love God above all else; to hope in Christ alone; and to believe God's Word without the shadow of doubt. Come, Holy Spirit.

694-696

Symbols of the Holy Spirit: water, anointing, fire

Anointing with oil: sign of the anointing with the Holy Spirit

1290-1294

Different Eastern and Western traditions of confirmation

Oil: sign of abundance and joy; of cleansing and healing

Postbaptismal anointing: sign of consecration and sharing in
the mission of Christ

Nothing in the Christian life happens without the strength
and fire of the Holy Spirit. Christ's followers can count on
the Spirit's presence as their unfailing inheritance. What Old
Testament men and women looked forward to is now ours in
Christ.

PRAYER: Lord, we dwell in you and you dwell in us by your
Spirit. Teach us to live a life worthy of your holiness.

697-701

Symbols of the Holy Spirit

Cloud and light: revealing, yet veiling, God's glory

Seal: the indelible mark of anointing with the Holy Spirit

Hand: healing, blessing

Dove: after the flood and at Jesus' Baptism

1295-1296

Seal of the Holy Spirit in confirmation: total belonging to
Christ

Christians are not simply a people who are supposed to obey a set of rules. They are a people whose lives have been made new by God's action within them. Christians have the teaching of Christ to guide them, but they also have the presence of the Holy Spirit in their hearts, teaching them the things of God.

PRAYER: My heart is set on you, O God, because you give me your Spirit. Awaken my soul each day to your grace.

---

## Saturday Week 38

742-747
The Holy Spirit:
   Conceived Christ in the womb of Mary
   Consecrated the Son of God for his mission as the Savior
   Builds, animates, and sanctifies the Church

1315-1321
Sacrament of confirmation
Essential link of confirmation with baptism

When Christ rose from the dead and ascended into heaven, he poured out the Holy Spirit into the hearts of his disciples. For us, too, "God has sent the Spirit of his Son into our hearts, crying, 'Abba! Father!'" (Gal 4:6).

PRAYER: Father, your Spirit teaches us everything. We know that we can do good only by his presence in our hearts.

## Sunday Week 39

**1297-1301**

On Holy Thursday the bishop of each diocese consecrates sacred chrism for use in confirmation

The celebration of confirmation:

Renewal of baptismal promises and profession of faith

Invocation of the Holy Spirit

Anointing with chrism on the forehead with the words, "Be sealed with the gift of the Holy Spirit"

Christians live Christ's new life by the grace of the Holy Spirit within them. The forgiveness of our sins and our incorporation into Christ makes us fit dwelling places for the Holy Spirit. In so many ways, both conscious and subconscious, the Holy Spirit inspires our daily growth in Christ.

PRAYER: Come, Holy Spirit, and fill my heart with zeal for God. Guide me to live like Christ.

## Monday Week 39

**1312-1314**

The bishop normally administers the sacrament of Confirmation

In danger of death, any priest can give confirmation

**1575-1580**

Bishops confer the sacrament of Holy Orders

Holy Orders is a sacrament limited to men

No one has a right to receive Holy Orders

Ordinarily bishops confer the sacrament of Confirmation, though a priest may do so in special situations. However, only a bishop can confer the sacrament of Holy Orders. The bishop's special position as successor of the apostles means that his role in these sacraments demonstrates how close the recipients are, each in their own way, to the heart of the Church.

PRAYER: Lord Jesus Christ, you are uniquely present to us in the person of the ordained. Through them, give us the grace to open our hearts to all you want to give us.

## Tuesday Week 39

268-274
God Almighty: nothing is impossible with God
God is infinite in mercy
When God seems absent
Faith glories in weakness

2777-2778
Bold and filial trust in God

God wants us to be so confident in him that we boldly expect him to provide all we need. He wants to supply everything for us, even beyond our expectations.

PRAYER: Father, you care for all our needs. You feed and clothe us. You give us what we need to find our way to you in heaven. We praise you for your great love.

2142-2145

Second commandment: the name of the Lord is holy

Respect for God's name is respect for God himself

Adoration and respect for the name of our Lord Jesus Christ

232-237

The mystery of the Most Holy Trinity is the central mystery of the Christian faith and life

The Trinity is a mystery that our reason alone could not discover

God's holy name is the name in which we are baptized. We ourselves come to bear his mysterious and awesome name as his children. The second commandment, to keep his name holy, indicates that we, too, insofar as we are his, are holy and are to live holy lives.

PRAYER: Holy, holy, holy is the Lord God Almighty. O God, may your name be known and revered by all.

2146-2155

The second commandment forbids the abuse of God's name

Blasphemy against God, Christ, the Church, the saints, sacred things

Pledging oneself by oath to commit evil deeds is contrary to the holiness of the divine name

Oaths in court and perjury

It is an offense to verbally associate God with one's own evil purposes and deeds. Even to fall into a habit of casual reference to God for the trivial affairs of life is a lack of respect for our divine Lord. Honoring God's name in every way is the appropriate response for all men and women.

PRAYER: Bless the Lord, the God of all. May all peoples honor and glorify your name, O God our Lord and Father.

## Friday Week 39

**2156-2159**
Baptism in the name of the Father and of the Son and of the Holy Spirit
Baptismal names for Christians

**2663-2664**
The Church's many ways and means of prayer

**2670-2672**
"Come, Holy Spirit"
The Holy Spirit is the Master of prayer for Christians

The Father, Son, and Holy Spirit are constantly with us in our Christian life. In something as simple as the Sign of the Cross and in something as life-changing as baptism, we constantly refer to the three members of the Trinity. This is the God in whose image and likeness we are created.

PRAYER: In the name of the Father and of the Son and of the Holy Spirit. Lord God, my life is entirely yours.

275-278
Nothing is impossible with God
God's power in his mercy

2160-2167
Second commandment: respect for God's name
Blasphemy, false oaths, perjury, swearing
Baptismal names and patron saints
Sign of the Cross
God calls each one by name

God himself is the pearl of great price. Nothing in this world compares to him. His name is all holy. Creation was made for his glory, and it tells the wonders of his name. Catholics recall his holiness, and his gift of holiness to them, each time they make the Sign of the Cross.

PRAYER: In the name of the Father, and of the Son, and of the Holy Spirit. Amen.

**430-435**
The meaning of the name Jesus, the name above every name
God, present in his Son, intends to redeem us from our sins
All men and women can call on the name of Jesus, and only
    Jesus, for salvation
At the heart of Christian prayer: The name of Jesus

At the name of Jesus every knee will bend and every tongue confess that he is Lord over all creation. And his lordship is not one of domination but one of deliverance from evil. Even the Father testified to him: "This is my beloved Son, with whom I am well pleased" (Mt 3:17).

PRAYER: Jesus Christ, may your name be known by every man and woman on earth, that all may be saved.

**185-188**
Common language of faith
Professions of faith: creeds, symbols of faith

**949-953**
Communion in the faith, in the sacraments, in charity
Communion of charisms

Christians are called by Christ to love all men and women. At the same time, their relationship with Jesus Christ gives them a unique and close relationship with each other, a "communion in the faith." Even the variety of their gifts and abilities is planned by God as a beautiful harmony in which everyone needs and serves the others.

PRAYER: Father, thank you for giving me wonderful friends in Christ. Thank you for the saints who have gone before us, leaving a magnificent testimony to your greatness.

---

## Tuesday Week 40

**425-429**

Proclaiming Jesus Christ in order to lead others to faith

To catechize is to reveal the person of Christ and to help others enter into the joy of communion with him

Catechists teach as spokesmen for Christ, who is the real teacher of everyone

**461-463**

Belief in the Incarnation is the distinctive sign of Christian faith

The followers of Christ today still recognize him as fully God and fully man. It is a joy to spread our knowledge of him to others. The more we know him, the more we are able to give him away.

PRAYER: Jesus, you asked the apostles, "Who do you say that I am?" With Peter, we proclaim: "You are the Christ, the Son of the living God" (Mt 16:15, 16).

436-440

Christ means Messiah, or Anointed

Anointing: the sign of consecration for a divine mission

Christ, the Holy One of God, anointed by the Father with the Holy Spirit

The true meaning of Christ's kingship is revealed on the cross

Israel expected God to send a Messiah—someone anointed with God's power to save them and to establish God's kingdom in their midst. This Messiah did come, but God's plan was not only to save Israel but to save the entire human race. Now his Messiah has died and is risen. He is restoring all mankind to a relationship with God.

PRAYER: God, you have vindicated your Son Jesus Christ by raising him from the dead. Fill our lives with the light of your Messiah.

446-451

The New Testament calls the Father "Lord" and calls Jesus "Lord"

Jesus' divine sovereignty over nature, illness, demons, death, and sin

The power, honor, and glory due to God the Father are also due to Jesus

Christian prayer is characterized by the title "Lord"

Many people have been deeply moved when they realized the significance of saying "Jesus is Lord." Jesus had power not only when he walked the earth, but even today he is Lord of each man and woman and he guides history from heaven at the Father's right hand.

PRAYER: Jesus, our Lord and Savior, you raise up the downcast; you hold us in the palm of your hand. May we glorify you by our holy lives as your disciples.

---

## Friday Week 40

---

65-67

Christ the full Word of God; there will be no further revelation
Private revelations
Sects with new revelation that claim to surpass Christ are in error

422-424

The Word became flesh
Peter's confession: "You are the Christ, the Son of the living God"

Always at the center of God's plan and God's work there is his only Son, Jesus Christ. The relationship of the Father and the Son is a great mystery. Christ, fully God, receives all from his Father, and when he comes into our world he brings us all from God, leaving nothing out. No one can ever surpass him.

PRAYER: Lord Jesus Christ, I turn to you. I believe that you are the One who was to come into this world to restore all mankind to God. I love and adore you.

452-455
Titles of the Second Person of the Trinity: Jesus, Christ, Son
  of God, Lord

479-483
The Son of God became incarnate
Jesus is true God and true man
One person, two natures

The Son of God, who dwelt in majesty with the Father, was willing to humbly come to us in weakness. He who was immortal was willing to come to us as one who could die. Without losing his divine nature, he became a man so that we could become the sons and daughters of God.

PRAYER: Lord Jesus, when we see you, we see the Father. You know him from before the world began, and you make him known in our world. May your light shine in the heart of every man and woman.

**522-524**
Christ's first coming, prepared for centuries
John the Baptist, immediate preparation for Christ
Season of Advent: expectation of the Messiah

**705-708**
Need for the restoration of the likeness of God in mankind
Promise to Abraham: the descendant who is Christ

Once humanity lost its relationship with God, its destiny became shrouded in darkness. Even then God knew where he would lead us and how he would bring us back to himself. Now that Christ has come, we can trace God's actions in history to restore us to his likeness in the fullness of Christ.

PRAYER: In our joys and in our trials, O God, you are always faithful. Open our eyes and ears to your Son, Jesus Christ, that we may be pleasing to you.

**441-445**
Jesus Christ, only Son of God
Acknowledgment of Christ's divine sonship: center of the apostolic faith first professed by Peter
God the Father's voice from heaven declared Jesus to be his Son
Jesus' glorified humanity after the Resurrection manifests his divine sonship

Jesus, the Son of God, received everything from his Father. He received the fullness of divinity so that we say he was "begotten, not made." This divine Son of God, who loves and obeys his Father, is the very One who came into the world to lead us back to the Father.

PRAYER: Jesus, we bless and praise you, and give you thanks for restoring us to the Father.

---

## Tuesday Week 41

**464-469**

Jesus Christ, true God and true man
Heresies against the doctrine of Jesus, God and man:
    Gnostic, Nestorian, Arian, Monophysite
Mary, mother of the Son of God made man, is rightly called
    Mother of God

For the first four to five hundred years of Christianity there were many doctrinal difficulties about the identity of Jesus Christ. Some theories favored his divinity and weakened the truth of his humanity. Others favored humanity over divinity, or saw Christ as a unique being placed somehow between God and mankind. The Councils of Chalcedon and Constantinople put an end to these disputes and gave us the understanding that Jesus Christ was one person with two natures, the human and the divine.

PRAYER: Lord Jesus Christ, you became man to bring us a share in the life of the Trinity and so to glorify your Father. You are worthy of all our praise.

535-537

The Baptism of Jesus; Jesus allows himself to be numbered
among sinners

The Lamb of God who takes away the sin of the world

Through baptism the Christian is sacramentally assimilated to
Jesus in his earthly death and in his risen life

1223-1225

The Passover opened the fountain of baptism for all mankind

The act of pouring water over the head, the vestments of
the priest, the lighted candles—what could be the meaning
of these unusual actions and symbols? Without faith they
would be empty rituals. But our faith allows us to see all the
realities of the Baptism of Jesus in this action of the Church.
With him we are baptized for a life of holiness.

PRAYER: Father, you give us new life in the waters of baptism. Send your Holy Spirit to inspire us to live that new life
in abundance.

4-10

Catechesis: the Church's efforts to form disciples of Christ
The Church's growth depends on catechesis

1697-1698

Catechesis for newness of life in Christ
Catechesis of the Holy Spirit, grace, sin, and forgiveness
Catechesis centers on Jesus Christ, the Way, Truth, and Life

Catechesis is instruction in the Catholic faith and formation in the life of Christ. Many members of the Church do not adequately pursue this kind of formation. But it is just as necessary that those who are already Christian grow in Christ as it is that the gospel be preached to others.

PRAYER: Lord Jesus, I give thanks to you with my whole heart. You bring us all the truth of the Father. You bring us new life in your Holy Spirit.

---

## Friday Week 41

---

863-865

Fruitfulness of apostolate depends on union with Christ, the
source of all apostolate
Charity: soul of the apostolate

871-873

All Christ's faithful are called to share his mission
Rebirth in Christ gives equal dignity to all who build up the
body of Christ

The Church is the first to benefit when it carries out the mission of Christ. Our efforts to extend God's kingdom of love to more and more of the fallen human race strengthen us as members of Christ.

PRAYER: Father, your great love endures forever. Thank you for associating us with your Son in his work of love for all men and women on earth.

561-570

Christ's whole life teaches us:

Bethlehem

Nazareth

Temptation in the desert

The Transfiguration

The entry into Jerusalem

Death and resurrection

Christians speak of the "hidden life" of Christ at Nazareth, drawing many lessons from the little that Scripture says or implies about the time when Jesus lived with Mary and Joseph before his public ministry. Indeed, every aspect of Christ's life is a profound model for us to follow, living a life in imitation of Christ.

PRAYER: Lord, like Mary, we keep everything about you in our hearts. Your example sheds light that gives us happiness and wisdom for all the challenges we face.

531-534
The mysteries of Jesus' hidden life: silence, family, work
Jesus fulfills the fourth commandment: his obedience to his parents is an image of his obedience to God the Father

2598-2599
Jesus learned to pray from his mother, and from the prayer of Israel
Jesus' filial prayer to the Father springs from a secret divine source

Even the silence of Jesus during most of his life teaches us a great deal. He was not on earth to seek glory for himself but to serve his Father. Only when the appropriate time had come did he make himself known publicly. His humble service is an example for us to imitate.

PRAYER: Father, blessed are all who find their strength in you, as did your Son Jesus. It is better to follow your will than to seek the treasures of this earth.

2558-2561
The mystery of the faith is meant to be lived on the basis of a vital personal relationship with God in prayer
Our prayer is a response to God

1810-1811
Human virtues, acquired by education and persevering action, are elevated by divine grace

It is impossible to live as we ought without a profound relationship to God through Christ. The fallen state of mankind tends to encourage us to stray from God. The efforts we make to pray and to do good dispose us to receive abundant graces from God.

PRAYER: Lord, you search our hearts to see if we will open them to you. To you, our help in all things, we dedicate every breath, every thought, every act.

## Tuesday Week 42

**2562-2565**

Man prays from the heart, his hidden center

Christian prayer: covenant relationship between God and man in Christ

Prayer in the presence of, and in communion with, the Triune God

**2581-2584**

The prophets' mission to convert the hearts of Israel

Incidents from the life of Elijah, father of the prophets

The prophets' encounters with God in prayer

God still reaches out to us today to change our hearts. Just as the world was created by his Word, so his Word spoken to us in the Church still has the power to create our hearts anew.

PRAYER: Lord, Almighty God, I delight in your Word. Like Mary, I ponder it in my heart.

59-61
God chose Abraham to be the father of a multitude of
   nations
"In you all the nations of the earth shall be blessed"

2570-2573
God's promise and the prayer of faith like Abraham's
Drama of prayer: testing of faith
Jacob's prayer: wrestling with a mysterious opponent

Today the Jew, the Christian, and the Muslim all look to
Abraham as their father in faith. Abraham's example of faith
can hardly be surpassed. He left all to follow God, not knowing where God was leading him. He was even willing to sacrifice his only son, Isaac, expecting to receive him back from
the dead.

PRAYER: O my God, have mercy on our weakness as human
beings. How greatly you have loved us. May we respond to
you with a faith as full as Abraham's.

2578-2580
Samuel learned to pray in God's presence
David's prayer as the Lord's anointed, fulfilled by Christ
Prayer at the temple in Jerusalem

2629-2633
Prayer of petition: expression of our relationship with God as
   his dependent creatures

Prayer in the context of the new hope we have in Christ

The humble prayer of petition, presenting our many needs to God, puts us in the proper position to receive his grace. Christ said that just as we would give our children bread when they ask, so much more will God our Father hear and answer our prayers.

PRAYER: Father, you never turn me away. Give me all the graces I need to serve you.

---

## Friday Week 42

---

2585-2589
Psalms: masterwork of prayer in the Old Testament
In the psalms the Word of God becomes our own prayer
The simplicity of the psalms makes them valid for all times
Constant characteristics of the psalms: spontaneity, desire for
    God, distraught situation of the believer

Prayer is so central to the life of every man and woman that one entire book of the Bible is made up entirely of prayers. The psalms have been used by God's people in both Old and New Testament times. The more we grow in Christ, the more we find in these God-given prayers.

PRAYER: Praise God for his mighty deeds. Let all that has breath praise the Lord!

2590-2597
Prayer, mysterious encounter between God and man
The prayers of Abraham, Jacob, Moses, David, and Elijah
The Psalms: always suitable for prayer

2661-2662
Sources of prayer: the Holy Spirit, the Word of God, the liturgy, the theological virtues

Prayer is an expression of the fact that, through Christ, Christians enjoy a living relationship with the Father. All of life unfolds in the presence of the almighty and transcendent Creator who hears the prayers of our hearts.

PRAYER: Father, though we stray from you, you are never far from us. What a wonder it is that you would reach out to us and find us. We remember your great blessings and we are deeply grateful.

2650-2655
Holy Spirit: living water within our hearts, leading to prayer
Word of God: wellspring of prayer

1073-1075
Liturgy:
Participation in Christ's prayer and in God's love
Summit toward which all Christian activity is directed; fount from which all Christian life flows

Prayer is a special part of the personal encounter between God and mankind. The Holy Spirit at work in our hearts raises us up to God and opens us to the Father's love. Christ's life in us is the source of our desire to turn to God.

PRAYER: Father, allow us to turn to you and find you. Give us the gift of prayer.

2659-2660
We encounter God in the present
"Today!"—the Holy Spirit makes prayer spring up in us in the events of each day

2835-2837
Man does not live by bread alone
The Bread of Life: both the Word of God and the Eucharist

We no longer have the past, and the future is not yet given to us. We have only the present. What is more, God himself is always ready for us to turn to him. It is now, in the present, that we can know, love, and serve God.

PRAYER: Lord God, I lift my eyes and my heart to you. I know you love me, and that you are with me always.

---

## Tuesday Week 43

**2746-2751**
The prayer of the hour of Jesus: his priestly prayer inseparable from his Passover
Jesus' prayer extends until the end of time
Petitions of the Lord's Prayer: concern for the Father's name, zeal for his kingdom, and accomplishment of his will

**769**
The Church's earthly pilgrimage, time of trial and expectation

Christ's prayer continues in the Church throughout her pilgrimage to heavenly fulfillment. Everything comes back into union in the Church, and thus in Christ—but the task of completing that union goes on in struggles and trials until Christ comes again in glory.

PRAYER: Father, glorify your Son as he glorified you and protect us as his disciples in the midst of all our trials.

---

## Wednesday Week 43

**2732-2737**
Temptations in prayer
Prayers of petition and the struggle over whether we are being heard

Praying according to God's will
Praying with a divided heart

Praying regularly and persistently leads to growth in Christ. We need this growth to face the challenges of our lives and relationships. Without spiritual strength we are in danger of losing our relationship with God.

PRAYER: Lord, I come before you to give you my whole life. With you I know I am safe, and that even through trials, I have the hope of your faithfulness.

## Thursday Week 43

2709-2719
Contemplative prayer: seeking him "whom my soul loves"
Recollecting ourselves in God's presence
Silence in contemplative prayer
The night of faith: we must be willing to keep watch with Jesus

It is by the grace of the Holy Spirit that we love God. He himself moves our hearts to seek him as the greatest treasure of all. Thus, through prayer we build a solid foundation for our lives as Christ's disciples.

PRAYER: Lord, I want to know you more and more. I open my heart to you; come make your home within me.

## Friday Week 43

1427-1429
Christ's call to conversion to those who have not yet heard the gospel
Ongoing conversion in the life of the Church

2725-2728

Prayer: a gift and an effort

The spiritual battle of Christian life is inseparable from the battle of prayer

There is a need for ongoing conversion in our lives because we are not yet free of the world, the flesh, and the temptations of the devil. In this life, we do not arrive at a place where the struggle ends. We need to be prepared for a continual battle of turning from evil to Christ.

PRAYER: Lord, teach us to pray. Give us the trust, the humility, and the perseverance we need.

---

## Saturday Week 43

---

2644-2649

The Holy Spirit inspires prayers of blessing, petition, intercession, thanksgiving, and praise

2680-2682

Prayer addressed to the members of the Trinity
Prayer with Mary, especially the Hail Mary

Under the guidance of the Holy Spirit, who forms the life and activities of the Church, prayer is meant to permeate every aspect of life. In a special way, the Holy Spirit leads us to turn to God. He guides us to turn also to Mary with our petitions, glorifying God for all he has done for her and through her.

PRAYER: O Lord God, you hear us when we call to you. We see your gracious hand at work in every need, and we thank you for your great love.

## Sunday Week 44

1827-1829
All virtues are inspired by charity
Supernatural charity
Charity bears fruit

2742-2745
Constant prayer inspired by persevering love
Prayer and the Christian life are inseparable

All of Christian life and Christian prayer depends upon love. Motives not based on love lead us away from a genuine Christian life. The love of God—supernatural charity—leads us to a life of joy and service to God and others from a sincere heart.

PRAYER: Father, change my heart that it may be like yours. I come to you as a sinner in need of your mercy, yet confident because you are full of love and mercy.

## Monday Week 44

1803-1804
Virtue: habitual and firm disposition to do good
Moral virtue is acquired by human effort

2221-2224
The role of parents to morally and spiritually form their children
Parents must see their children as belonging to God

Our example as parents means more to our children than our words. On the basis of our good example, by God's grace, our words can then have a profound effect on our children.

PRAYER: Lord, uphold our family lives by your grace. Show all parents how to bring their children closer to you.

---

## Tuesday Week 44

1805-1809

The four cardinal virtues play a pivotal role for all other virtues

Prudence: discerning one's true good and choosing the right means of achieving it

Justice: constant and firm will to give what is due to God and neighbor

Fortitude: firmness in difficulties and constancy in the pursuit of good

Temperance: moderated attraction to pleasures, balance in the use of created goods

So central are the four cardinal virtues to all of life that knowledge of them is a must if we are to shape our own lives and influence others for the good. We will tend to be either prudent or imprudent, just or unjust, brave or cowardly, temperate or intemperate. Knowing how to grow in these virtues and avoid these vices is absolutely crucial to living a good life.

PRAYER: Father, we want to grow up into the fullness of your Son. Come, Holy Spirit, give us the power and zeal to imitate Christ in all virtues.

1812-1816

Theological virtues: faith, hope, charity—the virtues of soul by which we relate directly to God

Virtue of faith: commitment of oneself to God

Faith works through charity and without works is dead

2656-2658

Wellsprings of prayer, the theological virtues: faith in the Lord; hope in Christ's return; God's love poured out in our hearts

By faith we know the most important truths about God and his goodness to us. By hope we have a certainty that God will always bless us. By charity we value God above all else, and our neighbors as ourselves. These are the three things that last—and the greatest of them is love.

PRAYER: Father, when you speak to us you give us faith. When you promise to bless us you give us hope. When you love us we are made new and love you in return.

1817-1821

Hope: trust in Christ's promises

The hope of Abraham: origin and model for the hope of the People of God

Hope in the midst of trials, discouragement, and abandonment

Hope perseveres to the end

Hope is the gift of God that allows us to see our fulfillment in Christ ahead of time. We are like Abraham, who set out for an unknown land that God had promised him. Like him we hope in God to bring us to a fulfillment beyond our ability to ask or imagine.

PRAYER: O God, you have done marvelous things. You have been victorious over evil, even over our sins. We trust in your certain promise of salvation.

---

## Friday Week 44

---

218-221
God is Love
God's love: everlasting and given freely
We are destined to share God's love

1822-1826
Charity: to love God above all, and our neighbors as ourselves
Christ's new commandment of love
Christ's love for us while we were still God's enemies
Charity: the greatest virtue

As John the apostle grew older, his message seems to have become more and more simply focused on love. He had been "the apostle whom Jesus loved," and that special love shaped his vision. Under the guidance of the Holy Spirit, he gave us the simple yet magnificently profound statement: "God is Love."

PRAYER: Father, you have loved all men and women, even me. May I grow in your love—in receiving it and in giving it away to others.

1833-1845
Virtue
Four cardinal virtues
Moral virtues
Theological virtues
Seven gifts of the Holy Spirit

The theological virtues of faith, hope, and charity give us an ability to relate to God and to his truth, goodness, and steadfast kindness. The cardinal virtues of prudence, justice, fortitude, and temperance allow us to live wisely and righteously with our fellow men and women. The gifts of the Holy Spirit inspire us to serve God and to live fervently for him.

PRAYER: Father, above all, fill our hearts with love for you. We believe that you welcome all who turn to you, and we hold fast to the hope you give us that we will come to fullness of life with you in heaven.

**2184-2188**

Refraining from work or activities that hinder worship on the
Lord's Day

Sunday: dedicated to good works for the poor; to family and
relatives; to reflection and silence

Society needs to preserve the quality of the Lord's Day

**2447-2449**

The Church's constant preferential love for the poor

There will always be the poor: need for social structures to
care for them

Recognizing the Lord's presence in the poor

Sometimes nations care for their poor, but at other times
they neglect them. The Church's love for the poor has been
consistent throughout history. Even today, there are many
places on earth where the poor would be completely neglected
if it was not for the care given to them by the Church.

PRAYER: Lord, you take pleasure in all your people, even
those living in poverty and misery. We humbly ask you to
show mercy to all who are suffering physically or spiritually.

**638-640**

On the third day he rose from the dead

The Resurrection is an essential part of the Paschal mystery
of Christ

Christ's resurrection: a real historical event

The empty tomb

Our secular age often prefers to understand the world in a strictly material way, without reference to spiritual realities. It is also a scientific age, but science cannot by itself explain occurrences like Jesus' resurrection from the dead. Yet if God's mysterious power did raise Jesus from the dead, there would be observable material results like the empty tomb and encounters with the risen Jesus in bodily form. These physical results are as much a part of history as any other occurrence.

PRAYER: Lord Jesus, the chains of death could not hold you. We give our hearts to you because you tasted death to give us life.

## Tuesday Week 45

641-644

Appearances of the risen Christ to Mary Magdalene, to the other holy women, and to the apostles
A new era began on Easter morning
The Resurrection is a historical fact, not a symbolic idea

988-991

I believe in the resurrection of the body
Resurrection of the dead on the last day

Christ was the first to rise from the dead, and we also will rise as he did. Our destiny is to live forever with God in new heavens and a new earth, which will be physical as well as spiritual.

PRAYER: Father, this life weighs us down. When it comes to an end, be our rock of new life in your Son.

648-650

Christ's resurrection is an intervention of God in creation and history

Resurrection: union of the soul and body of Christ, which had been separated by death

997-1001

Our resurrection: God will grant incorruptible life to our bodies by reuniting them with our souls in the power of Jesus' resurrection

Resurrection of the dead at the end of the world

While some other religions believe in reincarnation in this world, Christians believe that we live one earthly lifetime, and that we will rise at the end of the world with real bodies, though we do not yet know what those bodies will be like. However, we know that we will be like Jesus, who is already risen, and that we will be with him, sharing his life within the Trinity.

PRAYER: Lord, you will deliver us from every evil. Guard us, hear our prayers, and save us.

# Thursday Week 45

651-655

Christ's death and resurrection free us from sin and give us new life

Christ's resurrection is the principle and source of our future resurrection

1994-1995

The justification of the wicked is a greater work than the creation of heaven and earth

Justification: birth of the "inner man," entailing sanctification of one's whole being.

The resurrection of Christ is his return to a new life after death and is also the source of newness of life for us. The remarkable change of character described by Christ in the Sermon on the Mount has been realized in the lives of the saints, and to a lesser degree in the lives of many Christians throughout history. This newness of life is open to us even now.

PRAYER: O God, you are gracious to us and forgiving. How great is your salvation, bringing us from the kingdom of darkness to the kingdom of your Son.

---

## Friday Week 45

---

645-647

Christ manifested his new risen body to his disciples

Christ's risen body is physical and real, yet also glorified.

Resurrection: not a return to the same earthly life, but passing through the state of death to another life beyond time and space

1002-1004

We have already in some sense risen with Christ, participating also in his death

On the last day we will appear with Christ in glory

"Your bodies are members of Christ"

Christianity is a religion of facts as well as a religion of meaning. When Thomas doubted Christ's reserrection he did not doubt the meaning of the Lord's life but the fact of his resurrection. When he realized the fact was true, he said to Jesus, "My Lord and my God!"

PRAYER: Christ, you now reign in heaven, where you ascended from this earth. Mercifully guide those on earth to find their way there with you.

---

## Saturday Week 45

---

**2189-2195**
Third commandment: Keep the Lord's Day holy
Sunday, the day of the Resurrection
Sundays and holy days of obligation
Mass attendance
Day of rest

As his creatures, we owe God homage and worship. To give us a way to fulfill our duty to him, God commanded that we observe one day in each week as a special time dedicated to him. Christians observe this Day of the Lord on Sundays, the day Christ rose from the dead.

PRAYER: Lord God, all creation belongs to you. We remember to dedicate it all to you when we come together to worship in the Eucharist. We join with all creatures to proclaim your greatness.

**1166-1167**

Sunday: the Lord's Day, day of the Resurrection

The Lord's Supper, center of the Lord's Day

**2174-2176**

The Lord's Day, day of Christ's resurrection, symbol of the new creation, the first of all feasts

For Christians, the Sunday celebration replaces and fulfills the Jewish Sabbath, which prefigured Christ

One day a week we observe as holy in a unique way. It is Sunday, the day on which Christ rose from the dead beginning the new creation. This day is linked with the special holy day of rest God observed after beginning the first creation.

PRAYER: Father, we offer you a sacrifice of thanksgiving, to give you the praise you are due. Remember us with all the graces of your salvation.

**345-349**

God rested on the seventh day; the Sabbath

The eighth day: day of Christ's resurrection

**2168-2173**

Third commandment: observe the Sabbath, the Lord's Day

The Sabbath was made for man, not man for the Sabbath.

Some of the greatest experiences for mankind on earth are experiences of the Lord's holy feasts. Think of Christmas and Easter—at church and at home. Each Sunday is also a commemoration of Easter. Time would be colorless and bleak without these days set apart as holy by God.

PRAYER: Father in heaven, may your glory come down into our midst as we celebrate your holiness and your works on our behalf.

---

## Tuesday Week 46

2095-2100
Serve God alone
Adoration: to praise and exalt God while humbling oneself
Prayer is indispensable for being able to obey God's commandments

2781-2783
Prayer puts us in communion with God

Christianity is a religion of living relationship with God. Christ was our model, living in constant communication with the Father and giving us an example of a life of prayer. Any Christian may begin at any time to have a relationship with God in prayer.

PRAYER: Your voice, O God, is majestic. Let us hear you, and in hearing you find the joy and meaning of life.

2115-2122
Confidence in God for the future
All forms of divination of the future are wrong, including recourse to demons, the dead, horoscopes, palm reading, omens, clairvoyance, and mediums
All practices of magic, sorcery, and spiritism are wrong

2784-2785
We are freely adopted by God but must work to grow as his children

True religion puts God first, with us in orbit around him as our source of life and meaning. He is the absolute who gives meaning to our lives in his service. The various forms of irreligion attempt to place the individual at the center, making use of God for one's own purposes or aggrandizement.

PRAYER: Father, we rejoice in you as our Creator. We celebrate your name and your glory.

200-202
One God over the whole earth, and all peoples
Jesus is Lord

2110-2114
"No other gods before me"
Superstition; polytheism
Idolatry: divinizing what is not God

The people of Israel heard the words, "Hear, O Israel: The Lord our God is one Lord" (Dt 6:4). Their belief in one God set them apart from the other peoples among whom they lived; and though human reason is able to conclude that there is only one God, still the fact that God revealed this truth makes it entirely secure for us and changes our lives.

PRAYER: Father, those who reject you and trust in some creature endanger themselves and walk in darkness. But those who hold fast to you find strength and wisdom for the trials of life.

---

## Friday Week 46

---

222-227
Belief in one God

2129-2132
You shall not make for yourself a graven image
The images of divinity permitted in the Old Testament were
    ones that symbolically pointed toward the incarnate Word
Veneration of icons is not contrary to the first commandment

The Scriptures speak in the strongest terms against fashioning idols to be man's gods. The folly of it is apparent, yet mankind has often done this kind of thing. Now with God's sure help we know who he is and our lives are solidly founded on the one true God.

PRAYER: Father, you have allowed us to see you in your Son Jesus Christ. Hold us fast until we see you face to face.

2133-2141
First commandment: no other gods
Faith, hope, and love
Adoring God and the duty of worship
Superstition, sacrilege, and simony
Atheism
Veneration of sacred images

It is hard to imagine that men and women could carve a piece of wood and then regard it as their god. At the same time, it is just as foolish for us to live as though God were so distant that he is effectively not part of our lives. No, God is as near to us as every breath we take and every thought we conceive. We owe him our faithful service since we are his creatures.

PRAYER: Lord, help me to dedicate my life to you, and never to give myself to pursuits that lead me away from you. I want to love you above all things.

## Sunday Week 47

198-199
God is the First and the Last
The Father, First Person of the Trinity
Creation, the beginning and foundation of God's works

2083-2086
First commandment: love and worship God
Man's vocation: to make God manifest in this creation

Since we come from God and are destined to return to God, the aspiration of our hearts always goes beyond the visible world to something greater. We will never be satisfied with anything short of God himself.

PRAYER: O my God, I love you with all my heart, all my soul, and all my strength. Grant that through all my seeking I may find you, my true joy.

## Monday Week 47

325-327
Creator of heaven and earth, of all that exists
The bond between heaven and earth, the seen and the
    unseen

1046-1050
Common destiny of the physical world and mankind in
    Christ
We do not know the time of the consummation of the world

Mankind occupies a unique place in creation, being the only creature that exists fully in both the physical and spiritual orders of being. In a mysterious way our fall tainted the whole of the physical world; our resurrection will mean the renewal of all creation participating with us in the glory of Christ.

PRAYER: Father, you are so full of love for us as we struggle with the difficulties of this life. You have created us to know you and to serve you, and you will raise us up to a life greater than we could ask for or imagine.

---

## Tuesday Week 47

---

328-336
Angels: spirits who are servants and messengers of God
Angels were created through and for Christ
Angels in the life of Christ and his Church
Guardian angels

The angels behold God and do his will. However, because the Son of God became a human being and brought us into the life of God, the life of sanctifying grace, human beings are destined for a state of being higher than that of the angels.

PRAYER: Angel of God, my guardian dear, to whom God's love commits me here, ever this day be at my side, to light, to guard, to rule and guide.

402-406

The consequences of Adam's sin

The universality of sin and death; the universality of salvation in Christ

For Adam's descendants, original sin is a state of sin, not a personal act of sin

Human nature has not been totally corrupted by original sin but has been wounded

Mankind as we know it now is not fully expressive of God's creative intention. We do not know what a world without sin would be like. But we do know that God has overcome sin in Christ and has promised to renew the whole creation, removing all the consequences of sin.

PRAYER: How beautiful, O Lord, it will be to dwell with you free from all sin. Strengthen us for the battle against evil until Christ comes again.

385

The Fall

Where does evil come from?

The mystery of lawlessness is clarified only by the mystery of Christianity

601-603

Christ died for our sins, which deserved the punishment of death

1992

All have sinned, and all may be justified through Christ

Unless we see the glory of Christ and the wonders prepared for us in him, we cannot realize how wrong are the ways of God's enemy, who tempted our first parents, Adam and Eve. When we see the glory of Christ we can say: O happy fault that merited for us so great a salvation.

PRAYER: Father, let not your enemy rejoice over us. Where he has sowed hatred, bring a harvest of love and joy.

---

## Friday Week 47

---

1667-1673

Sacramentals: sacred signs that aid us in receiving the effects
    of the sacraments
When the laity, and when the clergy, administer sacramentals
Sacramentals do not confer grace but prepare us to receive it
    and dispose us to cooperate with it
Exorcism

There is scarcely any aspect of life for which the Church does not give us a sacramental blessing to help us live it in a holy way. From the blessing of a fishing fleet, to the religious profession of a nun, to the Sign of the Cross with holy water, we lift up our hearts to God aided by the sacramentals of the Church.

PRAYER: Lord, we turn to you in every part of our lives. Come and make us holy and pleasing to you.

350-354
Angels
Creation, destined for the good of mankind
Mankind, destined for the glory of God

413-421
God did not make death
Satan and the evil spirits
The fall of mankind and original sin
Christ has set us free from sin

The Church and the Scriptures assure us of the existence of angels, who are a very real help to us though we do not see them. They are creatures of God, and with the rest of creation they proclaim his glory and his wonderful deeds. On the other hand, the angels who sinned against God became evil spirits. The most powerful of these is Satan, who led mankind into sin through our first parents.

PRAYER: Father, by saving us from sin and joining us to your Son, Jesus, you have claimed us for your glory. We join with the angels in praising you forever.

337-344

God created the visible world to praise him
God's creative Word drew the world out of nothingness
Each creature possesses goodness and perfection
The interdependence and hierarchy of creatures
Man is the summit of creation

For all his creativity, man still draws entirely on what nature gives. Man's creations transform nature but remain within the limits of what God has put there. God, on the other hand, created a beautiful and harmonious universe from nothing.

PRAYER: Lord, the heavens tell your glory and the earth shows your handiwork. We join them in singing your praises, O Loving Creator of all.

2500-2503

Truth is beautiful in itself
Man expresses the image of God by the beauty of artistic works
Art bears a certain likeness to God's creative activity
Sacred art draws men to adoration, prayer, and love of God

There are great depths of mystery and beauty in this creation and its relation to the Creator. As man perceives these wonders, he is endowed by God with the ability to express them in various ways with his artistic abilities, which are given him to serve God and others.

PRAYER: How great are your works, O Lord. Put it in our hearts to worthily reflect them to your honor and glory.

---

## Tuesday Week 48

2464-2470
The eighth commandment forbids misrepresenting truth in our relationships with others
God is the source of all truth and calls us to live in truth
Man by nature tends toward the truth
Truth is necessary for men to be able to live with one another

Jesus is God's Word, and so he is the Truth because God is true. As he brings the kingdom of God, it restores truth among men, and when we encounter the truth he brings, it is natural that we will respond with a genuine love of the truth.

PRAYER: Lord, I love your Word. Always be my help, for I choose to live by your truth.

---

## Wednesday Week 48

2475-2479
False witness and perjury
Respect for the reputations of others
See your neighbor favorably

2488-2492

Rights to know are not unlimited

The sacramental seal of confession

Professional secrets

God directs us not only to avoid falsehood but also to communicate the truth. Many times withholding truth can be as harmful to others as lying itself. At the same time, communicating something when another does not have the right to know it can be harmful. Charity guides us in deciding which circumstance calls for which action.

PRAYER: Lord, there are so many times that people are hurt by lies and deception. Help us to trust in you and to rely on truth in our relationships with others.

---

## Thursday Week 48

---

2480-2487

Offenses against truth: flattery, boasting, lying

The purpose of speech is to communicate truth

1459-1460

Repairing the harm of our sins against others

The sinner must recover full spiritual health by making amends through penance

God created us to be interdependent, and thus truth between all men and women is absolutely crucial. Lies can damage people as much as physical injury can. Thus the life of each person is affected by the reliability, or lack of reliability, of others with whom he or she associates.

PRAYER: Father, uphold us in your truth. Let us walk in integrity of heart, with sincere love for all.

2493-2499

Society has a right to information based on truth, freedom, justice, and solidarity

Consumers of media need to practice moderation and discipline, resisting unwholesome influences

Journalists are obliged to serve the truth in charity

Civil authority needs to regulate media for the common good

2525-2527

Purifying the social climate from eroticism and voyeurism

Moral permissiveness: erroneous conception of human freedom

The work of the communications media is a great opportunity to aid society and individuals in finding truth and justice. Yet the media are so often misused that some conclude their existence itself is evil. Indeed, they can be used for evil, but they are given by God to be used for good.

PRAYER: Father, increase the presence and effectiveness of those who would use the media in the service of truth and love.

2504-2513

Eighth commandment, against false witness

Truth in deed and word

Martyrdom as a witness to the truth

Sins against truth

Sacred art

The Christian as a follower of Christ lives in the truth. Truth enlightens the mind and makes human relationships possible. It is only the revelation of God's truth that permits men and women to understand themselves and their own destiny, for Jesus says, "I am the way, and the truth, and the life" (Jn 14:6).

PRAYER: Lord Jesus, may your light enter my heart wherever there is darkness and sin. Your words are always true and reliable; I want to build on them as the rock of my life.

**2284-2287**

Scandal: an attitude or behavior that leads others to do evil

Scandal can be a grave offense, especially when given by those in authority

Scandal can come through laws or institutions, by fashion or opinion

**2292-2296**

Scientific research requires respect for moral criteria

Organ transplants require informed consent and must not endanger the life of the donor

Everyone needs to be careful not to give scandal to others. Our actions, just or unjust, are examples to others. They are occasions for us to encourage others to do good, or to tempt them to do evil.

PRAYER: Lord, guide us as a society to put just laws in place, that all may be encouraged by them to live righteously.

**1868-1869**

Cooperation in the sins of others

Social "structures of sin"

**2274-2279**

Protection of the embryo from the time of conception

Respect for the weak and handicapped

Direct euthanasia is morally unacceptable
Ordinary and extraordinary means of medical care

The removal of legal protections for the weakest members of society—the child in the womb, the old, the frail—has led society to increasingly accept the evils of abortion and euthanasia. It becomes a social habit, a "structure of sin," to disregard the destruction of those who do not have the power to speak for themselves.

PRAYER: Lord, help us overcome our habits of sin. Open our eyes as a society to justice and truth.

---

## Tuesday Week 49

---

2258-2262
Human life is sacred because of its relationship to God, the
    only Lord of life
The prohibition of murder is universally valid
Christ forbids anger, hatred, and vengeance

2280-2283
Suicide is contrary to the love of self, God, and neighbor
Voluntary cooperation in suicide is contrary to the moral law
We should not despair of the salvation of persons who take
    their own lives

The fifth commandment, "You shall not kill," forbids suicide as well as murder. Christ teaches us that the profound meaning of this command includes a prohibition of all ways of acting against the life of our fellow human beings, such as anger, malice, and disdain.

PRAYER: O God of life, we are grateful to you our Creator and Protector. Give us your own heart of love for others.

## Wednesday Week 49

2263-2267

Legitimate defense of persons and societies is permitted, and may even be a duty

Defense of one's own life does not make a person guilty of murder

Public authorities should limit themselves to bloodless means of punishment if they are sufficient

2297-2298

Kidnapping, hostage taking, terrorism, and torture are all morally wrong

In past times the Church did not protest the cruel practices used to maintain law and order—she now works for their abolition

Civil authorities are given a responsibility by God to maintain justice and peace in society. In those roles they legitimately punish wrongdoers. However, modern means give those authorities more scope to achieve their task without using some of the extreme measures of the past.

PRAYER: Lord, grant us times of peace, that we may freely grow in your grace. In times of hardship give us wisdom to be able to relate to others with mercy.

2270-2273

Human life must be protected from the moment of conception

From its earliest days the Church has forbidden abortion

The Church attaches automatic excommunication to the offense of cooperation in an abortion

The rights of the person are constitutive of civil society and its laws

The great evil of our times is legalized abortion. So many forces push for more and more free access to abortion that it can seem like this evil will never be reversed. But we can pray and work for change, confident that the truth will eventually prevail.

PRAYER: Lord, have mercy on us. Deliver us from evil. Help us to stand against all expressions of the culture of death.

## Friday Week 49

2299-2301

Care of the dying

Respect for the bodies of the dead

Autopsies and cremation

1684-1690

Funeral rites express the Paschal character of the Christian death

Communion with the departed in the Eucharist

Christ gives hope to the hopeless. It is only in him that the great mystery of death is overcome. The Church is present to console the loved ones of the person who has died and to point us on to eternity, where our loved one has preceded us.

PRAYER: St. Joseph, foster father of Jesus Christ and true spouse of the Virgin Mary, pray for us and for the dying of this day.

---

## Saturday Week 49

---

2318-2330
Fifth commandment, against murder
Sacredness of human life from conception to natural death
Legitimate defense
Sins against life: abortion, euthanasia, suicide
Leading others into sin
War and the arms race

Human life, in the image and likeness of God, is sacred. Each person is made by God and for God. "God alone is the Lord of life from its beginning until its end" (*Donum Vitae*, introduction, 5). Thus, we have no right to take the life of any of our fellow creatures.

PRAYER: Lord of all mankind, we have come to know your love. Let it overflow in our hearts for the sake of others.

1749-1754

Man is a moral subject whose acts are good or evil

Good intention does not make evil behavior good

Circumstances can increase or diminish the goodness or evil of an act

1790-1794

Human beings must obey their consciences

Conscience can remain in ignorance, which is often the person's responsibility

Men and women are corrupted by their own free acts of evil, but they also grow in virtue by the proper exercise of their freedom. Both good and evil become easier to do based on previous actions.

PRAYER: God, you are good to those who act rightly, but you hinder the ways of those who are evil. Happy are those who live their lives for you.

1730-1738

Freedom to act or not; to shape one's own life

Freedom grows as one does good

Sin is an abuse of freedom and is slavery, not freedom

1993

Cooperation between God's grace and man's freedom

Our freedom as human beings is a great sign of our high dignity. Each person shapes his or her own life by the use of freedom; what we value by our choices changes us for good or for ill. Though others can have a great influence on us, still we ourselves finally determine the outcome of our lives.

PRAYER: Lord, if you had not helped me by your grace, surely I would have strayed. Help me seek your honor and glory in all my actions.

---

## Tuesday Week 50

---

587-591
Jesus came to an Israel that had faith in one God and Savior
Jesus' role in forgiveness of sins was a stumbling block
Those who do not see their sin are blind
Jesus' claims to divine identity

1441
Jesus forgives sins and gives the same power to others

The difficulties of accepting the divinity of the man, Jesus, were certainly great. In fact, only the grace of God could make it possible to believe that he was divine. In a similar way in our day, only the grace of God allows us to see the unique presence of God in the human and divine institution of the Church.

PRAYER: Lord, to whom else could we go? You have the words of eternal life. Continue to open our hearts more profoundly to you.

**574-576**
Jesus was opposed because of his words and deeds
Sign of contradiction
Jesus seemed to be acting against essential institutions of
  Israel

**597-598**
Jews are not collectively responsible for Jesus' death
All sinners are authors of Jesus' passion

Jesus' divine way of acting is meant to open our hearts to repentance. But if human beings hold on to their sins then they find the encounter with Jesus to be threatening rather than consoling. Thus Jesus said, "Blessed is he who takes no offense in me" (Lk 7:23).

PRAYER: Lord Jesus, you come that the blind may see, lepers may be cleansed, and the lame may walk. Heal the hardness of our hearts that we might fully accept you.

**1739-1742**
Man's freedom is limited and fallible
Man freely sinned; wretchedness and oppression followed

**1949-1953**
The moral law is the work of divine wisdom and fatherly
  instruction

Moral law finds its fullness and unity in Christ

It is hard to understand that law and grace are not opposed to freedom. Yet the freer we are, the more sensitive we are to God's grace; and the law directs us only to do what is good, which is exactly what our freedom is given to us to achieve.

PRAYER: God, your truth and your law are established forever. May we grow in them every day.

## Friday Week 50

1755-1756
Some acts are always wrong
It is an error to judge acts only by intentions

1783-1789
Education of the conscience: an indispensable lifelong task giving freedom and peace
The Word of God: light for the conscience

Our culture has elevated choice to the highest possible status, as if it did not matter what the person chooses. All that seems to matter is the act of choice itself. Yet the Church teaches us that what we choose can please or displease God, and that it is by well-formed consciences that we make choices worthy of our dignity as his sons and daughters.

PRAYER: Father, guide me through the temptations that come when others call good evil and evil good. Your righteousness is my joy.

1757-1761
Object, intention, and circumstances of human actions
The end does not justify the means
Some acts are always wrong

1771-1775
Human passions
Reason and will determine good and evil, not the passions
Virtue and vice

Humans live in a state of weakness, in which our passions can cloud our judgment about good and evil. We need the guidance that comes from Christ's teaching about right and wrong. His teaching is a channel that guides us in the right direction when our own judgment would lead us astray.

PRAYER: Lord, you care for us as a vine dresser tends his vines. Even when you prune, it is so that we might bear more fruit. When we follow your laws we bring glory to your name.

**717-720**

John the Baptist, filled with the Holy Spirit even from his mother's womb

John completes the cycle of prophets begun by Elijah

**2683-2684**

The cloud of witnesses who have preceded us into the kingdom

The various spiritualities of the saints from the one light of the Holy Spirit

If John the Baptist was the beginning of the restoration of the divine image in man, then all the saints who have followed are the flowering of the divine presence of the Holy Spirit poured out by Jesus Christ. These are our fellow men and women, our true companions on the journey to heaven.

PRAYER: Father, you have given us great witnesses of your glory and of the power of your Holy Spirit. Give the graces in our own time that will lead many to become saints to bring honor and glory to your name.

**827-829**

The Church is at once holy and in need of purification

All members of the Church must admit they are sinners

Canonized saints and the Most Blessed Virgin Mary

957-959

Communion with the saints joins us to Christ
The offerings we make for those who have died
The one family of God

The Church is one, on earth, in purgatory, and in heaven—
one in Christ. The saints are now our companions, and we are
companions of our loved ones being purified in purgatory.
Trials on earth cloud our vision at times, but we are encouraged by the testimony of this great cloud of witnesses.

PRAYER: Father, we join all our brothers and sisters in
singing your praises and proclaiming your steadfast love.

---

## Tuesday Week 51

---

823-826

Though imperfect, the Church is unfailingly holy; Christ
    makes her so
All are called to holiness
Charity is the soul of holiness

946-948

The communion of saints
The good of each member in the body of Christ is communicated to the others
The riches of Christ are communicated to all the members

The more we consecrate our lives to God alone, the holier
we become. Our brothers and sisters in Christ have preceded
us on this path, and God calls us to follow them. His love
and care guide us each step of the way.

PRAYER: Praise the Lord Jesus Christ, our King now in
heaven. Let all that has life and breath praise the Lord.

**2101-2103**
Vow: deliberate and free promise to God, an act of devotion

**1973-1974**
Evangelical counsels: to remove whatever hinders the growth of charity

**925-929**
Missionary work requires the presence of the religious life
Secular institutions—state of consecration "within the world"

The history of the religious life is a remarkable tale of great saints and heroic deeds done out of love for Christ. Those who embrace poverty, who do not marry for the sake of the kingdom, and who offer their lives in obedience for the Church have been the source of unmeasurable blessing for the history of the world and the salvation of souls.

PRAYER: Lord, those who associate themselves with you flourish and bear fruit for others. Send graces for the vocations of many to religious life.

## Thursday Week 51

**1716-1717**
The Beatitudes
The Beatitudes depict Jesus Christ and his charity, and thus they also depict the Christian life

**2443-2446**
God blesses those who aid the poor

Christ's followers are recognized by their care for the poor

Love for the poor is incompatible with immoderate love of riches

To withhold necessities from the poor is to steal from them

We each have a need for, and therefore a right to, property, but at the same time the goods of the earth are intended by God for the use of all. Our choice concerning the goods of this earth is to use them just for ourselves or to also use them to serve others.

PRAYER: Lord, all that I have is yours and I am yours. May the Church never forget the great number who suffer so much from poverty and want.

---

## Friday Week 51

---

1720-1724

The happiness to which God calls man: kingdom of God; vision of God; joy of the Lord; God's rest

We are in the world to know, love, and serve God and so to come to paradise

Happiness is found in God alone

The paths that lead to the kingdom of heaven

Our true homeland is heaven, and we cannot find the meaning of our lives without a relationship of love with God our Father. No matter how many ways we avoid God, at the end of our journey he will be there. May we come to that point ready to happily meet him, acknowledging our need for his mercy.

PRAYER: O God, you established a covenant with us in Christ your Son. May we live faithfully according to that covenant, finding our joy in you.

---

## Saturday Week 51

---

1725-1729
The Beatitudes
The beatitude of eternal life
The beatitude of heaven

1743-1748
Human freedom
Responsibility

Eternal happiness consists in knowing God. He is the pearl of great price for which it is worth selling all else. We are wise if we turn from the passing treasures of this earth to the treasure that will never pass away.

PRAYER: Father, it is our great dignity to freely come to you. You have made us to seek truth, and we find it in you.

**487-489**

God's Son received a human body through the free cooperation of a creature, Mary

Holy women of the Old Covenant prepared for Mary: Eve,
Sarah, Hannah, and many others

**496-497**

The virginal conception is a divine work that surpasses all
human understanding

We honor Mary because of her role in the life of Christ
and therefore in our own lives. Since Christ came into the
world through her, we believe her role extends as far as his
does. His role in our salvation is decisive, but it is not independent of hers. Her assent to God opened the door so that
he could come into our midst.

PRAYER: Hail Mary, full of grace, the Lord is with you.
Blessed are you among women, and blessed is the fruit of
your womb, Jesus.

**490-493**

"Full of grace": God's gifts to Mary

Immaculate Conception: Mary was redeemed from the
moment of her conception

**1987-1991**

The grace of the Holy Spirit cleanses us from sin

The Holy Spirit works conversion in our hearts

Mary was redeemed from the moment she was conceived, saving her from all sin. Our redemption comes after we have borne original sin in our hearts. The glories of Mary's sinless state show us where we are headed in Christ.

PRAYER: Lord, have mercy on me a sinner. Mary, Mother of God, pray that we might become worthy to be your children in Christ your Son.

---

## Tuesday Week 52

---

**494-495**
"Let it be done to me according to your Word"
Mary gave herself fully to her Son to serve the mystery of redemption
Mary is truly Mother of God

**963-965**
Mary, Mother of Christ, mother of the Church
Mary's role in the Church flows from her union with Christ
Mary's prayers aided the beginning of the Church

Mary was prepared by the grace of God to receive the message of the angel. The good of the whole world hung in the balance that day as her response in faith opened the door to our salvation through her Son. She became not only the mother of the Son of God but of all the members of his Church.

PRAYER: Mary, Mother of God and our mother, pray for us. We dedicate our lives to honor you and to serve your Son.

**498-499**

Objections to the doctrine of the virginal conception of Christ

Christ's birth did not diminish Mary's virginity

**501**

Mary's spiritual motherhood extends to all whom her Son Jesus came to save

**2617-2619**

*Fiat:* Behold the handmaid of the Lord

Mary, the new Eve, at the cross

Mary's Magnificat

Mary's entire life was offered to God, to serve him as he wanted. In light of the redemption that would be accomplished by her Son, she was without sin and completely ready to receive God's message to her through the angel.

PRAYER: "My soul magnifies the Lord, and my spirit rejoices in God my Savior" (Lk 1:46-47).

**500**

The Scripture mentions "brothers and sisters" of Jesus who are not children of Mary but close relations

**2207-2213**

Family: original cell of social life

Family: place to learn morality and to begin to honor God

Society's responsibility to support and strengthen marriage and family

Scripture says that the Lord sets the solitary in families. It is his plan to have us live in the bonds of love and commitment to one another, the kind of bonds one finds within the family. The recognition of the importance and dignity of each individual person is, in fact, best achieved within the family.

PRAYER: Lord Jesus, come and dwell within my family. Let us know the joy of your presence in our midst.

---

## Friday Week 52

---

**502-507**
Christ's virgin birth manifests God's absolute initiative in the Incarnation
Mary's virginity is the sign of her faith

**922-924**
Christian virgins live for the sake of the kingdom of heaven
Virgins: consecrated to God, betrothed to Christ, dedicated to the service of the Church
The order of virgins

The witness of women remaining virgins in a unique dedication to the Lord has been inspired in the Church by the Holy Spirit since the beginning of Christianity. Mary herself was a virgin with her heart set totally on God. Her witness and that of other consecrated virgins is a sign in the Church that all Christians belong uniquely to Christ.

PRAYER: Mary, you had the great joy of becoming Christ's mother and ours. Pray for us, that our hearts might become more like yours—totally dedicated to the Lord.

## Saturday Week 52

508-511
Mary, Mother of God, preserved from all stain of original sin
Mary, ever-virgin and New Eve
Mary's yes in the name of the entire human race

973-975
Mary's *fiat* at the Annunciation
Mary taken body and soul into the glory of heaven
Mary's maternal role continues in heaven

By the grace of God, Mary freely assented to be the mother of the Son of God. The first Eve turned away from God in disobedience, but Mary, the New Eve, offered herself to be the handmaid of the Lord.

PRAYER: Mary, full of grace, intercede for us. We trust your care for us as a mother whose only interest is in the will of Jesus. We join with you to do whatever he asks.